EDITOR: Maryanne Blacker

DESIGN DIRECTOR: Neil Carlyle

• • •

ASSISTANT EDITOR: Judy Newman

DESIGNER: Robbylee Phelan

SUB-EDITOR: Mary-Anne Danaher

ARTIST: Louise McGeachie

SECRETARY: Wendy Moore

• • •

FOOD CONSULTANT: Vicky Liley

CONTRIBUTORS: Jacqueline Paradise,
Sheridan Rogers, Lynne Testoni

STYLISTS: Karen Byak, Francesca Dougall,
Jacqui Hing, Rowena Sheppard

PHOTOGRAPHERS: Gerald Colley,
Rowan Fotheringham, Andrew Payne, Stuart Spence

ILLUSTRATORS: Skye Rogers, Sue Ninham

COSTUMES: Sue Cadzow, Julie Palmer,
Vicki Rowston, Ann Rattey, Betty Smith

DIAGRAMS BY: Bill Murphy

• • •

PUBLISHER: Richard Walsh

DEPUTY PUBLISHER: Graham Lawrence

ASSOCIATE PUBLISHER: Bob Neil

• • •

Produced by The Australian Women's Weekly
Home Library
Typeset by Letter Perfect, Sydney.
Printed by Dai Nippon Co Ltd, Tokyo, Japan
Published by Australian Consolidated Press,
54 Park Street Sydney
Distributed by Network Distribution Company,
54 Park Street Sydney
Distributed in the U.K. by Australian Consolidated Press (UK)
Ltd (0604) 760 456. Distributed in New Zealand
by Netlink Distribution Company (9) 302 7616. Distributed
in Canada by Whitecap Books Ltd (604) 980 9852.
Distributed in South Africa by Intermag (011) 493 3200.

• • •

Kids' Parties

Includes index.
ISBN 0 949128 36 8.

1. Childrens' Parties. (Series : Australian
Women's Weekly Home Library).
793.21

• • •

COVER: Masked Mayhem, page 34.
OPPOSITE: Up, Up and Away, page 15.
BACK COVER: Clockwise from top: Teddy Bear's Picnic,
Dragon's Den, Twist and Shout.

KIDS' PARTIES

Childrens' parties really are quite magical. A cake laden with candles, a tribe of boisterous friends, party food and fun costumes are ingredients for success. In each chapter you'll find ideas for invitations, decorations and costumes plus fabulous food that will tempt the fussiest eater and satisfy the most adventurous. We have divided the book into four age groups and suggested five themes for each group. But feel free to mix the themes around to suit your child.

BRITISH & NORTH AMERICAN READERS: Please note that conversion charts for cup and spoon measurements and oven temperatures are on page 127.

Photography: Rowan Fotheringham; Styling: Rowena Sheppard

UNDER 2 YEARS

With tiny tots, partytime success is summed up in the "Three S" rule – keep it short, simple and stimulating. Aim to keep the party to a 1 to 2 hour limit – any longer and you're sure to have more than one crying and cranky tot on your hands! Times for an infants' party should be governed by sleep times; for 1-year-olds you may be able to sandwich in the festivities between morning and afternoon naps while 2-year-olds might be best entertained from around 3pm. (This late afternoon timeslot also has the advantage that older, school-aged children will be on hand to help if necessary.) If in doubt, consult the guests' parents.

✳ It has been said that the best formula for a child's party is to invite the same number of guests as the number of the birthday – but a first birthday isn't likely to be much fun with only one guest, is it? Consider how big your house is and how well your child gets on with others before deciding on numbers – you don't HAVE to invite every child in the playgroup ... there will be enough of that sort of trauma once your child starts school!

✳ Three or four children is a good number for tiny tots – and parents! – to handle without creating too much havoc. Request that a parent remains with the child for the duration of the party as even the most outgoing tot can suddenly have a screaming need for mummy or daddy when the excitement gets too much! Always have some adult refreshments on hand to entice parents to stay. It also pays to enlist the help and support of grandparents – their experience and patience can be invaluable assets, especially if there's a squabble brewing!

✳ Set boundaries within the house and/or garden. Close off all bedrooms – including your child's – and lock the doors if necessary. Try to make "off limits" rooms as unattractive as possible by hiding or camouflaging temptations such as the television and video recorder – your adult helpers will come in handy for this.

✳ Minimise the damage to carpet from spills by laying down plastic sheeting – especially under the food table and entry and exit passages. Nature isn't always obliging with sunny skies and firm ground underfoot. So if you are planning an outdoor party, ALWAYS have an indoor alternative on standby.

✳ Use your commonsense with decorative objects around the house. Remove all such temptations to a safe place or higher ground to avoid squabbles and embarrassment. No-one likes to spoil a party with a spanking!

✳ Ensure that all entry and exit ways are secured – check your house with military-style precision for escape routes. It's worth it for peace of mind as some toddlers are true Houdinis of the house!

✳ Ask parents to BYO bottles or trainer cups – not too many under-2s can successfully master a cup or mug without creating a diabolical mess! Invest in a couple of packets of disposable paper bibs that can be whipped off, thrown away and replaced without much fuss or expense and save on soiling special party clothes.

GAMES

Bear in mind that children under 2 really have no concept of structured party games so you can put away the Blind Man's Bluff blindfold and Pin The Tail On The Donkey set for a few years. These young party goers will be happy with some bright, happy songs to *"dance and sing"* to, whistles, rattles, balloons and streamers. And don't expect them to be quiet and well-behaved while everyone sings *"Happy Birthday"*! You might like to make a cassette recording of favourite nursery rhymes and silly songs, or invest in one of the many children's recordings readily available over the counter. Ask other parents if you can borrow recordings for the day.

Get the children in a circle and go through the actions with them for *"Ring a Ring a Rosie"*, *"I'm a Little Teapot"*, *"Mulberry Bush"*, *"Bananas in Pyjamas"* or *"Three Blind Mice"*.

One traditional party game that might work is Musical Cushions. Have one less cushion than children. Children walk around the cushions to music, when the music stops everyone tries to sit on a cushion. The child that misses out then selects a cushion to take out and sits on the outside of the circle. The game continues until there's one child and one cushion left.

RIGHT: Clockwise from back left: Teddy's Picnic Cake, Chocolate Bear Cookies, Grizzly Bear Bread, Cheesy Bears.
Large teddy bears: Teddy Bear Shop. Medium teddy bears: Toyworld. Picnic rug: Avalon Village Living

TEDDY BEARS' PICNIC

Who hasn't, at one stage or another, been besotted by the humble teddy bear? There's something about this most loveable, likeable character – an intangible charm that more often than not allows him to become a child's closest "friend" ... a friendship that may well carry over through the teen years and into adulthood.

So it's only fitting that this fine, furry chum should have his very own party – better still, a fun-loving, frolicking picnic! One of the biggest pluses about giving your child a teddy bears' picnic is that each little guest is encouraged to BYO teddy – a factor which may make them feel more at home and secure within what may be unfamiliar surroundings. Tots under 2 will almost certainly respond favourably to a party that involves their favourite cuddle buddy.

If the weather is suitable, plan to make it a true picnic – lay down a large, waterproof groundsheet and cover it with a brightly checked cloth or blanket; pick a nice, shady spot under a tree on the lawn or in a nearby park. Alternatively, you could still create a picnic atmosphere inside your house by laying the party table out on the floor.

INVITATIONS

Instead of issuing the invitation in your child's name, use his or her teddy's name instead. It could read something along these lines:

"Edward T. Bear requests the pleasure of the company of Barney B. Bear and Samantha at a very special picnic to celebrate Oliver's birthday."

Or for a more informal approach:

"PSST! Hey! Have you heard? Oliver's having a birthday! And to celebrate, we're having a picnic for all his special friends … and their teddies, of course! You're invited!

Make your own teddy-shaped cards or use brightly coloured paper with teddy stamps all over it. But don't fret if you haven't got the time or the energy … there's plenty of commercially manufactured invitations available featuring the ubiquitous teddy!

DECORATIONS

If your picnic is outdoors, there's little need for extravagant decorations aside from a few balloon bunches and maybe a streamer decorated tree. You might also like to make a tree in your garden the focal point for gift wrapped goodies – let the children scour it and discover its treasures! Be sure to give each guest and their bear a name tag – you will have to consult parents before the party as to any special names the teddy may have been "christened" with!

And it goes without saying that there must be a place at the picnic for each guest and teddy plus some special teddy bear hats and paper bibs – at least one cuddly companion is sure to be "offered" some cake and ice-cream!

GAMES

Another good way to get teddy and the children well and truly involved in the party is to play dress ups – provide a big basket full of doll's or baby's clothes including caps, scarves, jumpers, jackets, socks and bow ties, and let each child learn how to get their bear into some glad rags! They'll have a ball trying to dress them up and their antics will certainly keep the adult observers amused!

GOODY BAGS

When all the little teddy bears and friends have eaten their fill and tired themselves out for the day, have on hand some special picnic bundles to take home; pack up a selection of delicious teddy bear biscuits, a rubber teddy stamp and perhaps a bright new ribbon for each bear to wear, into a checked handkerchief bundle tied onto a jumbo pencil. Label these goody bags "The Bear Necessities" or "The Bear's Bundle"!

GRIZZLY BEAR BREAD

12 slices brown bread

butter for spreading

½ cup crunchy peanut butter

½ cup honey

100g dark chocolate

50g white chocolate

red and blue food colouring

Lightly spread bread with butter. Spread each slice with peanut butter and honey.

Melt dark chocolate over pan of hot water, spoon into a greaseproof piping bag. Pipe bear faces onto each bread slice.

Melt white chocolate over pan of hot water, divide into two even portions. Add a few drops of red food colouring to one and blue colouring to the other until chocolate turns pale pink and pale blue; mix well. Spoon into two separate greaseproof piping bags, pipe blue bows under half the bear's faces and pink on the remaining faces. Chill bread until chocolate sets.

Makes 12.

CHOCOLATE BEAR COOKIES

125g butter

½ cup castor sugar

1 egg, beaten

1¾ cups self-raising flour

2 tablespoons cocoa

Choc Bits

Cream butter and sugar together until light and fluffy. Add egg, beat well. Fold in sifted flour and cocoa. Turn mixture onto a floured surface, knead lightly. Roll out thinly. Using a large round cutter or the base of a drinking glass, cut biscuit mixture into rounds. Place onto greased oven trays. Cut the same number of small rounds, cut each small round in half and use as ears on each bear face.

Decorate each cookie with Choc Bits for eyes and nose.

Bake in a moderate oven for 12 minutes. Allow to cool on trays.

Makes about 12.

RIGHT: Chocolate Bear Cookies.

CHEESY BEARS

12 slices white bread

butter for spreading

12 cheese slices

1 tablespoon Vegemite

Place bread onto cutting board, lightly butter each slice. Top each slice with a cheese slice.

Using a teddy bear cookie cutter, cut a bear shape from each bread slice. Spoon Vegemite into a greaseproof piping bag. Pipe teddy bear faces onto cheese. Chill prior to serving.

Makes 12.

Note. Teddy bear cutter available from kitchen speciality shops.

TEDDY'S PICNIC CAKE

2 x 340g packets chocolate cake mix

1 quantity Vienna cream, see glossary

green food colouring

1 cup green coconut, see glossary

small square checked material

2 small toy bears

assorted sweets

plastic dolls furniture

Make cake following directions on packets. Spread mixture into 2 x 20cm greased square cake pans. Bake in a moderate oven for about 40 minutes or until firm; cool on wire racks. Position cakes on prepared board, join with a little Vienna cream. Tint remaining cream light green. Spread cream evenly over sides and top of cake. Coat top and sides of cake with coconut. Decorate cake with remaining ingredients.

BEAR BIB

50cm green cotton interlock fabric

3 brown felt squares *or* 30cm brown felt

1 red felt square

30cm fusible webbing

black fabric paint

Make pattern following diagram. Cut bib from fabric using pattern. Cut 4cm-wide fabric strips for binding outer and neck edges of bib. Cut four 32cm x 4cm for bib ties. Cut five bears from brown felt and five bow ties from red felt following diagram. Cut same number of bears and bow ties from webbing.

Join binding strips to give desired lengths for outer and neck edges of bib.

With right side of binding facing wrong side of bib, stitch binding to outer edge of bib. Turn binding over to right side of bib, fold under a narrow hem on raw edge and stitch binding to bib. Repeat for neck edge.

Turn in 5mm along edges of bib tie pieces. Fold in half lengthways, wrong sides together, stitch close to folded edges. Pin pairs of ties to each side of bib, one on front and one on back. Stitch in place on wrong side of bib fabric.

Fuse webbing to wrong sides of bears and bow ties. Peel off backing then fuse bears onto bib in desired positions. Repeat for bow ties.

Outline bears and bow ties with black fabric paint. Allow paint to dry.

TEDDY BEAR EARS

10cm fur fabric or fur scraps

35cm length pantihose

Make pattern following diagram. Cut four ears from fabric using pattern.

Place two ear pieces right sides together, stitch around edges leaving lower edge open. Trim, neaten and clip seam. Turn right side out, stitch a small pleat then zigzag lower edges together. Repeat with remaining ear pieces.

Fold pantihose strip in half lengthways, stitch together at ends to form loop. Pin lower edges of ears into fold of pantihose band, stitch in place.

ABOVE: Teddy's Picnic Cake.
FAR RIGHT: Bear Bib, Teddy Bear Ears.

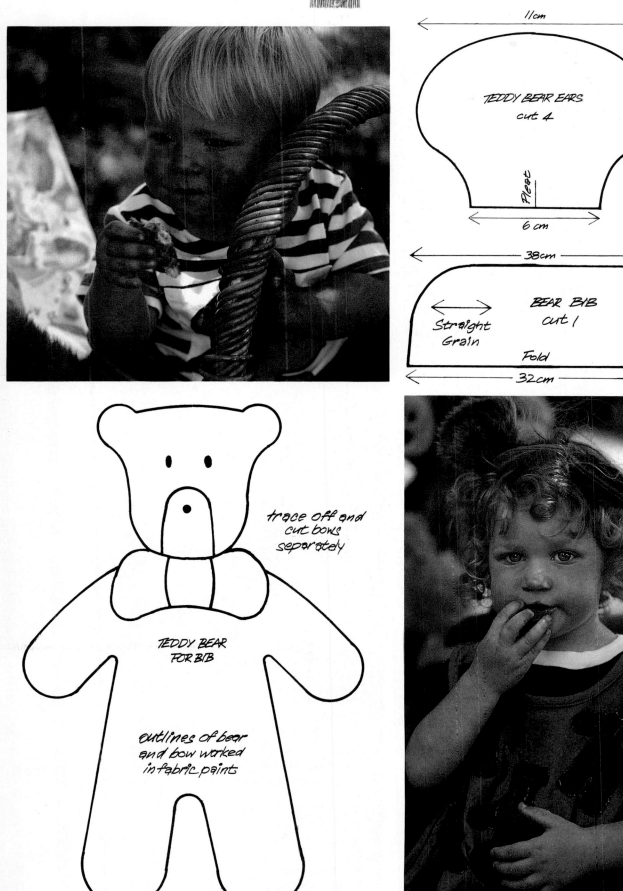

TEDDY BEAR EARS
cut 4

11cm

10cm

6 cm

Pleat

38cm

BEAR BIB
cut 1

Straight
Grain

Fold

Fold

9cm

trace off and
cut bows
separately

TEDDY BEAR
FOR BIB

outlines of bear
and bow worked
in fabric paint

9

COLOUR YOUR WORLD

The essence of this concept is visual appeal ... a very important aspect for littlies! But there's much to be said for single colour parties for you too – they're so easy to prepare and great fun to watch!

All you need to decide is which colour you and your child like best then set about devising a menu and decorations. And even though the tots may be too young to know just which colour has been chosen for them, the spirit and visual impact will not be lost on them. Who knows, your one colour party may prove to be educational as well as enjoyable.

Here's a sample of some classic one colour party concepts you might like to try.

RIGHT: Clockwise from front: Perfect Pink Necklaces, Pink Fairy Bread, Pretty in Pink Dolly Cake, Butterfly Dreams.

Chairs & table: Ikea. Tea set: Fidelity Traders. Antique cloth: Avalon Antiques. Balloons & streamers: Carnival and Toy Wholesalers

Now here's a party scheme sure to appeal to the little girl in all of us! Even the tender under-2s will respond to a fantasy of pink froth and bubble, sugar and spice.

INVITATIONS

While the colour theme should certainly dominate, you may choose to introduce an extra colour-keyed concept ... such as a pink elephant party, perhaps? Ask guests to don their prettiest pink party outfit and get the parents into the act as well – even if a Dad is to be the accompanying parent, he should be able to wear something pink ... a shirt, tie or maybe socks!

DECORATIONS

Like all good parties, balloons should abound – you may be able to pick up a selection of various pink shades or add white balloons for contrast. If you're following the pink elephant theme, be sure to fashion a set of cardboard cut-out "ellies" to adorn the party table, doors and doorways – even the front gate!

FOOD

From fairy floss to fairy bread, let pink rule! Use a splash of cochineal to blush up plain white icing for cup cakes and lemonade; serve strawberries (check for allergies first) both sliced and in milkshakes as well as pinwheel ham sandwiches and luscious chunks of watermelon. And the cake? Make it a paragon of pinkness! Festooned with flowers – fresh from the garden or concocted from confectionery.

COSTUMES

Coordinate hats but don't expect tots to take to them straight away – you may need to wear one (and be sure to issue them to attending parents, too) until they come around! Alternatively, pin a pink blossom or bow in each guest's hair.

GOODY BAGS

Look around your supermarket for inexpensive pink purses as a change to the conventional paper bag; fill them with musk sticks, marshmallows and coconut ice as well as a pretty pink surprise ... why not a tiny fluffy pink elephant, a necklace of threaded pink sweets or maybe some pretty "play" lipstick?

ABOVE: Butterfly Dreams.
BELOW: Perfect Pink Necklaces.

BUTTERFLY DREAMS

12 very small scoops strawberry ice-cream

12 patty cake liners

12 ice-cream wafers

assorted pink sweets

Cut wafers with scissors to resemble wings. Place 1 scoop of ice-cream into each patty cake liner. Position a wafer on each side of ice-cream. Decorate with assorted sweets.
    Makes 12.

PERFECT PINK NECKLACES

2 punnets strawberries, hulled

½ watermelon, seeded

pink marshmallows

pink jubes

string

Cut watermelon into large cubes. Thread strawberries, watermelon cubes and sweets attractively onto string to resemble pretty necklaces. Tie ends of string in a bow.
    Makes about 6.

PINK FAIRY BREAD

12 slices white bread

butter for spreading

pink cake sprinkles

Remove crusts from bread, discard crusts. Spread bread lightly with butter. Sprinkle with cake sprinkles. Cut each slice into quarters diagonally.

Makes 48.

BELOW: Pretty in Pink Dolly Cake.

PRETTY IN PINK DOLLY CAKE

2 x 340g packets buttercake mix

red food colouring

¼ cup raspberry jam

250g pink prepared soft icing

1 doll

ribbon

lace

Make cakes following directions on packets. Add a few drops of colouring to cake mixture; mix well. Two-thirds fill a greased and floured Dolly Varden cake pan (10 cup capacity). Bake in a moderate oven for 50 minutes or until firm; cool on a wire rack.

Place cake on prepared board. Brush with warm jam. Roll icing out thinly to cover cake.

Insert doll in top, decorate with remaining ingredients.

Use the tops of fancy buttons to make impressions in icing, if desired.

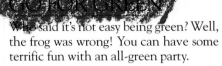

GO FOR GREEN

Who said it's not easy being green? Well, the frog was wrong! You can have some terrific fun with an all-green party.

INVITATIONS

Give guests the green light for adopting a suitably green theme – perhaps you could issue a lily pad shaped card for a green frog party or maybe ask them to come and spend the afternoon with the Jolly Green Giant! Remind them to wear something green.

DECORATIONS

Create your own green "pond" for the party with a drape of green felt or fabric – steer clear of crepe paper tablecloths as the dye may run all over your tiny guests should it get wet! Make cardboard lily pads as placemat alternatives and add a liberal scattering of jolly green jelly frogs.

COSTUMES

Provide some green laurels for children and adults to wear in their hair. (Green garden ivy loosely fashioned into circles looks great.)

FOOD

Edible greenery is easy to serve up to finnicky-to-feed tots – try tiny mashed avocado finger sandwiches, cheese-stuffed celery sticks and chunks of gorgeous green fruits such as honeydew melon, grapes and kiwifruit. Add a dash of green food colouring to apple juice for a healthy thirst quencher with a truly verdant hue! Your cake with a difference could be green (lolly) frogs sitting atop a lily pad of ice-cream – it's a treat that needs to be eaten without delay!

GOODY BAGS

After a round or six of "Ten Green Bottles", you can pack guests on their way with special green goody bags (if you've got the time and energy, make your own from cut-up green plastic garbage bags) brimful of jelly frogs and snakes, green jelly beans and a friendly frog memento ... of the fluffy toy variety of course!

YELLOW FEVER

Now, we're not suggesting for one minute that you devise a party around a deadly disease! The idea is to create a happy yellow party theme that's as bright as sunshine itself!

INVITATIONS

Spark off the golden theme with sun-shaped invitations asking guests to come in their sunniest and wearing their biggest smiles. Be sure to make it a gilt-edged invitation for fun!

DECORATIONS

Gild the house with big bunches of yellow balloons painted with happy faces and trailing golden streamers to resemble the sun. Even if the great outdoors hasn't blessed you with favourable conditions, at least everyone will be beaming inside!

COSTUMES

Present each child and adult with a lovely sunflower or piece of wattle to pin on their dresses or shirts.

FOOD

Plan your menu around a host of delicious golden fare including popcorn, pineapple, banana splits or sandwiches (cheese or honey, simple but jam-packed with toddler appeal), and wash it all down with apple juice or banana flavoured milk. For a fun base to your super sunshine cake, why not use a custard pie? Most tots just love the taste and texture of gooey custard! Let them tackle it with their fingers if you don't mind some sticky but harmless mess!

GOODY BAGS

Give guests a bag full of sunshine to take home – aside from the usual spray of sweets – yellow, no doubt – include a sunny, smiley face badge and a small pack of crayons so they can scribble their own sparkling day!

UP, UP AND AWAY

If there's one thing that symbolises fun and festivity, it simply has to be the humble balloon. A party just doesn't seem like a party unless the house is adorned with these big balls of colour, and children, in particular, just love them ... their glee and delight in these light-as-air playthings seems to be universal. A balloon party – featuring games and crafty ways with the rubber wonders – is a sure-fire yet inexpensive way to treat tots to an hour or so of uninhibited fun!

Firstly though, you should be warned that youngsters under 18 months of age may not appreciate the loud and often unexpected "pop" of balloons as they inevitably get squeezed, scrunched and rolled on. Closer to 2 years of age, children become more accustomed to the noise and actually seem to LIKE it! Perhaps though you should invest in ear plugs!

ABOVE: Clockwise from front right: Circular Sandwiches, Jelly Balloons, Popcorn Pleasures, Balloons Cake.
Multi-coloured helium-filled balloons with streamers and balloons on sticks: Mona Vale Balloon Company.
Paper plates, cups and party decorations: Carnival and Toy Wholesalers

INVITATIONS

Clever balloonophiles will spend some time writing the details of the invitation on a balloon; this is easier than it sounds as the secret is to inflate a balloon, write the details on it then let the air out. Pop the balloon into an envelope and mail. You might also care to include an instruction slip with the balloon such as:

"Blow me up and you'll find a special message just for you!"

Alternatively, draw different-shaped balloons on a piece of card, colour them and send them out as invitations.

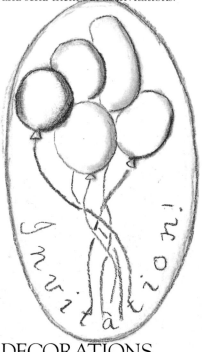

DECORATIONS

It goes without saying that you'll have to invest a few dollars in many, many packets of balloons. Bunch them into every corner, across each doorway and into crevices and cavities throughout the party room and rest of the house. Pay special attention to dressing up light fittings (not too close to the bulbs or wirings, though) and ceilings with masses of overhead colour; you may choose to fill these balloons with helium so they rise up apparently of their own accord. Contact a commercial balloon gas or party balloon supplier for more details.

Issue guests with special balloon hats – easily fashioned from the simple cone-style party hats with one or two balloons attached to the cone tip. Write the child's name on one of these balloons.

GAMES

The best decorations can be done by the children themselves so incorporate decoration and play by supplying the tots with readily inflated balloons – their little lungs couldn't cope with blowing up a balloon – plus a treasure trove of craft odds and ends such as stick-on stars, stripes, glitter, chunks of foil and crepe paper balls, ribbons, streamers, feathers and bows. Let them create fabulous glitzy masterpieces of balloon collage or encourage them to paint or draw funny faces to fabricate balloon people.

Of course, under-2s may not have the skill needed to hold a balloon and decorate it at the same time; a patient pair of adult hands will come in handy at this time so be sure to have plenty of helpers on standby.

Obviously there will be quite a bit of mess after this creative balloon-fest; be prepared by laying down a carpet of newspaper, plastic or cotton sheeting. Guests can be asked to bring their own smock or you can supply simple plastic bag popovers to preserve party gear.

Other nifty air-filled treats include unusually-shaped "sausage" balloons which nimble fingers may fashion into various animals and a big bunch of "Balloon Surprises" – balloons filled with tiny plastic toys, play jewellery, sweets and confetti. Do keep a watch over just what the children do with the small odds and ends and be sure they don't swallow anything inedible!

GOODY BAGS

Create miniature hot air balloon baskets filled with bright sweets (a balloon attached to a paper sweets basket), a special balloon with guest's name written in bright, glittery paint and perhaps a small bubble blowing game. And don't forget to give each child at least one or two decorative balloons to take home ... providing, of course, they haven't all been popped in the course of the fun!

RIGHT: Clockwise from back right: Balloons Cake, Circular Sandwiches, Jelly Balloons, Popcorn Pleasures.

CIRCULAR SANDWICHES

12 slices bread

butter for spreading

assorted toppings: chopped green jelly and peanut butter; hundreds and thousands; strawberry jam; blue cake sprinkles and cream cheese; cheese slices; mashed avocado and lemon

Cut bread slices into rounds with sharp knife or scissors (using a saucer as a guide). Spread with butter, decorate each with your selection of toppings.
   Makes 12.

POPCORN PLEASURES

3 cups coloured popcorn

200g white chocolate

½ licorice strap, cut into 6

Melt chocolate over hot water, add popcorn. Stir gently until well combined. Divide into 6 portions. Shape each into a ball. Place onto a foil lined tray. Insert one licorice piece into each ball, chill until firm.
   Makes 6.

JELLY BALLOONS

85g packet jelly crystals

¼ quantity Vienna cream, see glossary

12 plain sweet biscuits

Make jelly following directions on packet. Pour into a wetted or oiled deep muffin pan. Refrigerate until firm. Spread Vienna cream lightly onto each biscuit. Remove jelly from pan. Place one jelly onto each biscuit.
   Makes 12.

BALLOONS CAKE

2 x 340g packets buttercake mix

2 quantities Vienna cream, see glossary

food colouring, various colours

ribbon

toy clown

Make cakes following directions on packets. Spread into 2 greased 1 litre pudding basins. Bake in moderate oven for about 20 minutes or until firm; cool on wire racks. Place cakes on prepared boards. Divide Vienna cream into 2 even portions, tint desired colours. Spread one colour over each cake. Decorate with remaining ingredients.

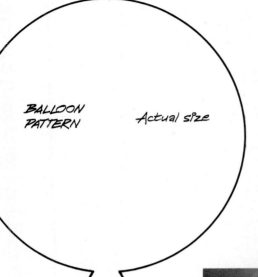

BALLOON
PATTERN   Actual size

BALLOON T-SHIRT

red T-shirt

3 x 10cm fabric pieces (green, yellow, blue)

10cm fusible webbing

black fabric paint

Trace balloon pattern. Cut one balloon from each fabric piece using pattern. Cut three balloons from fusible webbing.

Iron webbing to wrong side of each balloon piece. Peel backing off webbing, position balloons on T-shirt and iron to secure in place.

Outline each balloon with black fabric paint and draw strings down from base of each balloon. Draw a bow where they meet. Allow paint to dry.

LEFT: Balloons Cake.
RIGHT: Balloon T-shirt.

SANDPIT SENSATION

Everyone loves the beach ... including tiny tots! But for practicality and safety's sake, you're better off confining party festivities for the under-2s to the sandpit, where everyone, including Mums and Dads, can have a feast of fun in the sun!

A word of advice about numbers for a sandpit party: keep them low. Four to five children in the average sized sandpit is more than enough and if they're overcrowded, you can expect the squabbling to start very early in the day.

LEFT: Clockwise from front: Buckets of Colour, Chocolate Chip Cars, Sandpit Cake, Savoury Tubs.

Deck chairs (child size), picnic rug, beach towels: Avalon Village Living. Plastic toys: Toyworld and Fidelity Traders, Brookvale. Balloons and party decorations: Carnival and Toy Wholesalers

INVITATIONS

Put your imagination to work by issuing a novel invitation – perhaps you could buy up a bundle of bucket and spade sets and attach the invitations to them, requesting that each guest brings the set on the day, and hand deliver them. If this is a little difficult, why not draw a bucket and spade – writing the party details on the spade. Or if you'd prefer to mail the invitation, sprinkle half a handful of sand into the envelope before sealing ... the surprised invitees will have no doubt just what sort of party they'll be attending!

With the dress code for the sandpit being very informal (if anything at all!), let parents decide how they'll attire their youngsters – you might like to have on hand a big bottle of Factor 15+ sunblock and a couple of spare sun hats, however, as these sun screening essentials can easily be overlooked in the rush to get to the party.

DECORATIONS

Decorate a sandpit? Sounds like a tall order but there are ways to make it a bit more fun and interesting than your average, run-of-the-mill pit. Both boys and girls will willingly toddle on into a sandpit that's readily equipped with a special "mountain track" for heavy duty cars, trucks and plastic farmyard animals. Simply pile up the sand along one side of the pit, mould the track into the side of the "hill" and reinforce the lower edges with cardboard. You might like to pop in a few road signs, houses and bus stop shelters as well. Don't be too upset should the track disappear into the general sea of sand quite rapidly, however!

If you don't have a permanent sandpit fixture in your yard, consider converting a wading pool for the day ... better still, borrow a neighbour's or friend's and have two. ALWAYS check that the sand is reasonably clean and hazard free – the odd twig or leaf won't do too much harm provided there is plenty of parental supervision, but crawling nasties will! Spiders, lizards and beetles – even if they ARE of the harmless variety – will undoubtedly upset littlies, so rake the sand thoroughly just before the guests are due to arrive.

Anyway, the best surprises in the sandpit are the gift wrapped kind – not the crawling, creepy species! Wrap and bury some small sandy treasures for the children to discover as they dig about – plastic animals, moulds, bright flags and shells are ideal.

FOOD

You'll have to make the decision just when you'd like to serve your tiny guests the party fare – either before they hit the pit or after but absolutely NOT during! Have you ever encountered the gritty displeasure of sand in your sandwiches? If you choose to feed them beforehand, make sure the party table is out of sight of the sandpit as tots can conveniently forget the food and head straight to the fun instead. Once they've had their fill (keep the menu simple and non-sticky if possible) offer each child a damp facecloth to remove grease and found grunge – it's amazing how quickly sand will stick to grubby little bodies!

And as for eating after the fun and games, you run the risk of upsetting those who haven't quite finished creating the masterpiece castle or worse still, having a hungry but overtired brood on your hands! Maybe a splash under the sprinkler or in a wading pool would not only brighten them up but wash off the sand too.

GOODY BAGS

Take home goody bags can be replaced by inexpensive plastic buckets; pop in a pair of crazy kid's sunglasses, a pot of bright zinc cream or maybe a "Sandpit Survivor" certificate to commemorate the occasion. It's a party that's guaranteed to be full of nitty gritty fun!

SAVOURY TUBS

12 slices bread

melted butter

4 hard-boiled eggs, peeled, mashed

1 tablespoon milk

salt and pepper

½ cup shredded lettuce

Remove crusts from bread, discard crusts. Roll bread slices with rolling pin. Brush each side with melted butter, press firmly into deep patty tins. Bake in a moderate oven for 12 minutes or until crisp. Remove from oven.

Combine egg, milk, salt and pepper. Spoon into bread tubs. Decorate tubs with lettuce.

Makes 12.

BUCKETS OF COLOUR

24 small frozen shortcrust pastry cases

85g packet jelly crystals

assorted soft sweets

Place frozen pastry cases on oven trays. Bake in a moderate oven for 15 minutes or until golden. Remove and allow to cool in foil cases on a wire rack.

Make jelly following directions on packet, allow to chill slightly. Spoon partially set jelly into pastry cases, refrigerate until firm. Decorate buckets with sweets.

Makes 24.

ABOVE: Buckets of Colour.

CHOCOLATE CHIP CARS

125g butter

½ cup castor sugar

1 egg, beaten

2 cups self-raising flour

Choc Bits

Cream butter and sugar together until light and fluffy. Add egg, beat well. Fold in sifted flour. Turn mixture onto a floured surface, knead lightly. Roll out thinly. Using a car-shaped cutter or free hand, cut biscuit mixture into car shapes, decorate each with Choc Bits. Bake in a moderate oven for 12 minutes, allow to cool on trays.

Makes about 12.

SANDPIT CAKE

2 x 340g packets chocolate cake mix

1 quantity Vienna cream, see glossary

green food colouring

1 cup green coconut, see glossary

¼ cup apricot jam

1 cup brown sugar

plastic toys

assorted sweets

Make cakes following directions on packets. Spread mixture into 2 greased 20cm square cake pans. Bake in a moderate oven for 35 minutes or until firm; cool on wire racks. Place on prepared board.

Join cakes with a little Vienna cream, tint remaining cream green. Spread sides of cake with cream. Coat sides of cake in coconut. Brush top with warm jam, sprinkle with brown sugar. Decorate with remaining ingredients.

BLUE HAT WITH SHELLS

brightly coloured straw hat *or* natural coloured straw hat

can of blue spray paint (for natural straw hat)

shells (approximately 24)

hand drill (with fine bit)

2m matching narrow cord

If using a natural coloured hat apply spray paint and allow to dry.

Drill hole in each shell with hand drill. (Holes in small fine shells can be punched with a sharp needle.) Punch 3 holes in hat with skewer or scissors – one at centre back and one at each side.

Cut length of cord to fit around inside edge of brim. Thread one end of cord through hole in centre back and around brim of hat.

Thread shells onto cord and space as desired around brim. Thread other end of cord through hole at centre back of hat. Knot ends of cord together on underside of hat. (Thread shells onto two lengths of cord for extra strength, if desired.)

Cut two 50cm lengths cord for ties. Knot one end of each length, thread through side holes, from the top through to the underside.

Thread a shell onto ends of each tie and make a double knot to secure shells.

LEFT: Sandpit Cake.

HATS ON

Alice in Wonderland knew she'd stumbled onto something rather extraordinary at the Mad Hatter's Tea Party – so why not give your own out-of-the-ordinary tiny tot a hat party? It's a bright, easy and colourful way to let wee ones learn how much fun "dress ups" can be!

The best thing about a hat party is that you can let the children don as many different hats as you can beg, borrow or create.

RIGHT: Clockwise from front: Sweet Summer Hats, Savoury Quiche Bonnets, Cracker Caps, Fancy Hat Cake.

Striped fabric: Ikea. Plastic hats, balloons and party decorations: Carnival and Toy Wholesalers. Construction hat, fire helmet: Toyworld, Warriewood Square

INVITATIONS

Craft your own hat-shaped cards – a simple top hat would do nicely – and ask guests to bring a favourite piece of head-wear; Mums and Dads may come to the rescue with a cap or sunhat that may ordinarily be "off limits". Insist that all party attendees must bring (and preferably wear) a hat of some sort ... including all the parents!

DECORATIONS

Find the biggest, most outrageous hat you can and pin it to the front gate or door; bedecked with streamers and balloons, no-one will miss THIS party place! Good decorative hats include an over-sized sombrero (an often discarded souvenir from abroad) or broad brimmed straw sunhat.

The party table can feature hat-shaped placemats – be crafty and make a different one for each guest; write their name in the brim or band. Another clever party table hat trick is to turn inexpensive plastic or paper bowls into upside down hats and fill them with party food. Youngsters should, however, be discouraged from trying such head gear on before it's empty!

But of course the main decorations will be the hats themselves. Festooned with flowers (real or not), badges, tinsel, streamers, brimful of confetti, abounding with plastic animals or smartened up with sweets – each hat will be an enjoyable asset to the fun. Be prepared for the guest who prefers NOT to don a hat, however. Offer them special headwear options such as an American Indian-style feather band, an animal ear hat (rabbit or elephant are easy to fashion and look terrific), lace bridal veil or even a simple floral garland. All may meet with disapproval and tears so don't force the issue, just leave the tot alone and he or she may come around.

GAMES

Hat snatching will most certainly be the order of the day ... Cowboy Bill may get rid of his appearance and choose to adopt another role – perhaps that of Pirate Pete's. Should this in-fighting begin, initiate a game of hat-swapping, encouraging everyone to join in and therefore taking the sting out of the snatcher's antics! Turn on some music and get the children to play musical hats.

GOODY BAGS

It goes without saying that take home treats should be carried in a hat – an inexpensive and easy hat-bag is the pointed, cone-style party hat. Replace the elastic with ribbon or string as it may not be strong enough to withstand the weight of sweets and treats.

SAVOURY QUICHE BONNETS

2 sheets frozen shortcrust pastry

½ cup chopped ham

¼ cup chopped shallots

2 eggs, beaten

250ml thickened cream

salt and pepper

¾ cup grated cheese

Allow frozen pastry to thaw to room temperature. Cut into 6cm rounds (use a glass or pastry cutter). Line greased shallow patty tins with pastry.

Combine ham and shallots, sprinkle over pastry in base. Mix eggs and cream together, seasoning with salt and pepper, if desired. Spoon into pastry cases. Sprinkle with cheese. Bake in a moderately hot oven for 20 minutes or until golden. Serve cold.

Makes about 18.

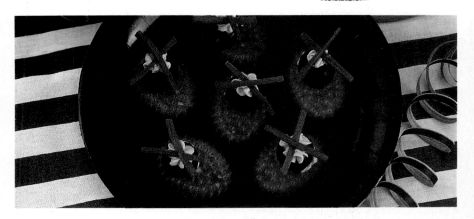

CRACKER CAPS

12 savoury biscuits

1 carrot

6 cherry tomatoes

1/3 cup soft cream cheese

Place biscuits on a serving board. Cut carrot into matchstick lengths, slice cherry tomatoes in half, spoon cream cheese into a small piping bag. Pipe a small amount of cheese onto each biscuit. Place a tomato half on top of each biscuit, pipe a small rosette of cream cheese on top of each tomato. Arrange carrot lengths on top of rosette to resemble fun sport hats.

Note. Additional topping ideas include: rounds of cheese, gherkin or boiled egg.

Makes 12.

SWEET SUMMER HATS

12 chocolate biscuits

12 marshmallows

1/2 cup raspberry jam

125g prepared pink soft icing

1/2 quantity of glace icing, see glossary

hundreds and thousands

Place biscuits on a board, place a marshmallow in the centre of each biscuit. Lightly brush marshmallow and biscuit with jam. Roll soft icing out thinly, cut fluted rounds to fit over biscuits, place icing over each biscuit. Tint glace icing if desired, place a small amount of glace icing sprinkled with hundreds and thousands on the side of each hat.

Makes 12.

FANCY HAT CAKE

3 x 340g packets buttercake mix

2 quantities Vienna cream, see glossary

yellow food colouring

ribbon

plastic or silk flowers

Make cakes following directions on packets. Spread mixture into a greased 1 litre pudding basin and a greased 23cm round cake pan. Bake in a moderate oven for 35 minutes or until firm; cool on wire racks. Place small cake on top of larger cake. Place on prepared board.

Join cakes with a little Vienna cream, tint remaining cream pale yellow. Spread over sides and top of cakes. Decorate with remaining ingredients.

LEFT: Sweet Summer Hats.
ABOVE LEFT: Cracker Caps.

PEG BUCKET HAT

50cm beige felt

50cm red felt

1 black felt square

20cm red gingham

2.8 litre beige peg bucket

craft glue

red thread

Cut circle of beige felt to fit bucket base. Measure depth and circumference of bucket. Using measurements, cut beige felt piece for side adding 1cm allowance to height. Cut cheeks and lips from red felt. Cut eyebrows, eyes, eyelashes, nose and mouth from black felt following face diagram, below left. Cut a long 2cm-wide strip of red felt to cover bucket handle. Cut two 20cm x 15cm gingham pieces, for bow. Cut 40cm x 1.5cm strips red felt, for hair.

Lay hair strips across base piece so they extend over the edges, attach to base piece by stitching through the centre of each strip. Stitch strips along top edge of side piece. Continue until the desired effect is achieved.

Glue side piece to bucket, fold over and glue 1cm allowance to bucket base.

Glue base piece to bucket and trim hair strips around front and on top to form fringe.

Glue felt face pieces in place (see face diagram, left).

Glue 2cm-wide red felt strip to one end of bucket handle, wind around handle and glue at other end to secure.

With gingham pieces right sides together, stitch around edges leaving an opening at one end.

Turn right side out, press, topstitch around edges stitching opening closed.

Sew two rows of gathering stitch through centre of bow across width. Pull up gathers. Cut a small black felt strip, wind around gathers and stitch ends of felt strip together. Handstitch bow to handle at centre.

PEG BUCKET HAT

ABOVE: Fancy Hat Cake.
LEFT: Peg Bucket Hat.

3 TO 5 YEARS

Now that they can walk, talk and pretty much think for themselves, the scope for good times, fun and games at a party for pre-schoolers is broadened considerably. By now, they've definitely got a notion about what they like and dislike and they've discovered how much fun being with other children can be. The world of fantasy has also opened up in a big way, prompting fertile young minds to adapt to play acting with ease.

✱ There are still limits to their patience and understanding of organised games and party structures, so themed parties, where their time is taken up with creative activity rather than a series of games are best to keep toddlers amused. They'll be determined to explore the new territory both within and outside the house.

Photography: Andrew Payne. Styling: Jacqui Hing

✱ Establish "off limits" zones (preferably under lock and key) and secure all entries and exits. Fiercely independent, most pre-schoolers will wander off if given the opportunity!

✱ You'll have a little more flexibility with party times as many pre-schoolers drop their daytime sleep by the time they're 3. However, do check with parents as some lucky Mums and Dads can still persuade their youngsters to partake in some daytime shut-eye!

✱ Music is now much more a part of the pre-schooler's day, so be sure to give them a wide variety of upbeat popular tunes as well as the nursery rhyme favourites. You may be able to work in a little classical concerto, too, especially if the party involves some sort of craft activity.

Encourage them to dance, sing and whistle as they go about their party business!

✱ Whatever your party concept, bear in mind at all times that you'll have on your hands a bunch of busy, enquiring, eager little minds with rapidly developing personalities. They can now express themselves when they're happy, sad, angry, elated ... their range of emotions runs high and low in a remarkably short space of time. Keep this uppermost in your mind and you'll be able to cope with the inevitable squabbles and woes besetting any group of youngsters. If you stay calm and concentrate on diverting attention away from any apparent crisis, the party will proceed without too much fuss or bother. And you may well survive to plan for another party, same time next year!

MASKED MAYHEM

The concept of the masquerade – where you deliberately cover up your true identity with a mask or costume – is centuries old. Lords and ladies of the grand royal courts of Europe were renowned for their fabulous masked balls and even today, the masquerade party is a popular favourite with party goers of any age.

Pre-schoolers will love this form of dress ups – especially if they get the chance to make their own mask. And you'll find it an ideal way to occupy those busy little fingers for a great deal of the allocated party time!

INVITATIONS

Set the stage with an invitation shaped like – you guessed it – a mask. Make your own and sprinkle with glitter or feathers. Simply draw a snappy looking mask onto cardboard and you or your child can colour it, or buy some inexpensive cardboard masks from the newsagent or stationers. Little boys may prefer a mask invitation fashioned after their favourite superhero such as Batman or The Phantom, while little girls may lean towards a prettier romantic mask invitation.

DECORATIONS

If you're not afraid of the mess kids make when they are creating, try this:

Prepare the party room as you would for any craft session by laying down protective sheeting over the floor and covering up any upholstered furniture. Gather together mask making essentials – brightly coloured sheets of cardboard (already traced with a series of mask outlines), lengths of ribbon or elastic to thread through the masks, play scissors, glue and sticky tape, felt marking pens, glitter pots or pens, lace, bright feathers, bows, buttons, shells, sequins, shredded cellophane, strips of foil ... the list is almost endless! Use just about any crafty material you can lay your hands on and pop them into a series of clean ice-cream containers.

Assemble the lot along a benchtop or around a trestle table. Instead of place cards, lay down a piece of the mask-traced cardboard in a spot for each child and write his or her name on it. Be sure that you have plenty of scissors and glue pots or pens to go around as well.

If the children are making the masks, let them create a mask that takes their fancy ... some may go for an outrageous invention crammed full of feathers and froth, while others may simply choose to colour theirs black and make their own mysterious statement! Help them thread ribbon or elastic to keep the mask in place and let them wear whatever mask they've made. Some guests may choose to lay their masterpiece aside to take home and show off – by all means, let them do so and offer them a stock mask to wear for the duration of the party.

If you want to steer clear of the mask making at the party, set the scene by decorating your home with fun masked figures – give each stuffed toy, teddy bear and doll a mask, fix a HUGE mask to the front door, pop masks on any lamp posts or garden fixtures (especially the gnomes!) and mask up the family pets! And don't forget to wear one yourself! Hopefully, most toddlers won't be frightened by your mysterious appearance ... if they are, quickly whip the mask off, show them who you are and offer their parents a store-bought mask to get everyone in the party mood!

LEFT: Clockwise from left: Masked Pizzas, Masked Cake, Funny Faces, Happy Cakes.

COSTUMES

Pick up some cheap masks from supermarkets or novelty party shops, or make your own. Scour magazines to find faces, eyes and mouths. Glue pictures onto cardboard. Cut out holes for eyes in full faces. Tape an ice-cream stick to the back of each mask. Add feathers or beads for effect.

We kept our mask shapes simple: a star with glitter, an orange pussycat with pipe-cleaner whiskers, a painted oval shape and a sequinned eye mask adorned with a feather!

You can make some terrific full face and full head masks from the humble brown paper bag. There's also more scope for adding lots of decorative bits to a bag-style mask including hair, hats ... even bow ties!

GAMES

● If time permits, start a fun game of story telling, asking the children to create a character for the mask they've made. Ask them questions such as where do they live, what is their job and what hobbies do they have. This will really get their imaginations working overtime!

● Another activity is to get children to draw masks onto balloons. Use thick felt pens and don't have balloons blown up too tightly! Children love this game.

GOODY BAGS

At the end of the day, send the mighty masked ones on their way with a goody bag full of masked party morsels, their special mask creation and perhaps a Polaroid snapshot of themselves dressed as a masked marvel ... a memento which most children will certainly treasure and sit proudly on display in their rooms.

RIGHT: Clockwise from left: Masked Pizzas, Masked Cake, Funny Faces, Happy Cakes.

MASKED PIZZAS

2 cups self-raising flour

salt and pepper

1 tablespoon butter

½ teaspoon dried mixed herbs

1¼ cups milk, approximately

¼ cup tomato paste

assorted toppings: sliced black olives, capsicum, cabanossi, salami and mushrooms

tasty cheese, grated

Sift flour, salt and pepper together in medium bowl. Rub butter in lightly with fingertips. Mix in herbs. Pour all the milk in at once, mix quickly with a knife and turn onto floured board. Knead lightly. Cut into six even-sized portions. Roll each portion into a flat round or cut with a large round cutter. Place on greased oven trays.

Brush pizza bases with tomato paste, add desired toppings to make a face. Sprinkle with cheese. Bake in moderately hot oven for 15 minutes or until golden brown.

Makes 6.

FUNNY FACES

12 slices white and brown bread

butter for spreading

assorted toppings: sliced ham, pineapple rings, cherry tomatoes, gherkins, sliced capsicum, carrot, alfalfa sprouts, cheese slices, avocado, sliced beetroot, lettuce

Place bread on serving platter. Lightly butter bread. Create funny faces using desired toppings.

Makes 12.

MASKED CAKE

2 x 340g packets buttercake mix

1 quantity Vienna cream, see glossary

red food colouring

assorted sweets

ribbon bow

coloured ball

plastic hair (cut from a toy mask)

Make cakes according to directions on packets. Spread mixture into 2 greased 20cm cake pans. Bake in moderate oven for about 35 minutes or until firm; cool on wire rack. Place cakes on prepared board.

Join cakes with a little Vienna cream. Tint remaining cream pink. Spread cream evenly over cakes; decorate with remaining ingredients to resemble a face.

HAPPY CAKES

340g packet chocolate cake mix

24 paper patty cake liners

1 quantity Vienna cream, see glossary

food colouring, assorted colours

assorted sweets

Make cakes according to directions on packet. Place paper patty liners in muffin pans. Fill patty cake liners ⅔ full with mixture. Bake in a moderate oven for about 20 minutes or until firm; cool on wire rack.

Tint Vienna cream in desired colours, decorate cakes with cream and sweets to resemble happy faces.

Makes 24.

MASKS

We made our masks from coloured cardboard and decorated them with paint, glitter, tinsel, sequins, cotton wool (dyed with paint), curling ribbon, streamers, feathers and felt pens.

Cut a cardboard shape to fit the child's face or use a plain purchased cardboard mask as a base. Our masks included stars, fish, wacky looking characters and a comical clown – anything is possible, just let your child's imagination provide the design.

EASY AS A,B,C

Every parent knows that the grounding for a good education begins long before their child takes those first memorable steps inside the school gate ... the pre-school years are vital building blocks to basic comprehension and learning.

An alphabet party is a great way to teach toddlers the fundamentals of letter identification – without the formality of books and other conventional teaching resources. Educationalists have long recognised the value of making learning fun ... and it's amazing just how much children can learn when they actually enjoy it!

Most children in the 3 to 5 age bracket will be familiar with certain letters and associate them with everyday objects. Whether it's A for apple or Z for zebra, they will often identify several letters quite easily. Take advantage of this and let your child choose which letter to celebrate at their party ... hopefully, they won't have their heart set on an awkward one such as X or Q! If you do encounter this problem, gently suggest that perhaps an "S" party might be more fun as there are more delicious foods and interesting costumes beginning with the letter S than the letter X!

Of course, you may choose to centre your alphabet party around your child's first initial – such as a "J" party for James or an "R" for Rebecca. This may be more fun and appropriate for older pre-schoolers who are starting to assert themselves and gain some idea of self identity.

Whatever letter you eventually choose, be sure to reinforce its use and role at the party – label each dish of food and give the children name tags such as "Danny the pirate" or "Sally the cowgirl". You might also like to decorate the party room with bright drawings of objects starting with the celebrated letter.

"P" PARTY

INVITATIONS

Write the invitation on the back of a home-made P plate or make one from green cardboard cut in the shape of a pea, or write on a paper plate!

COSTUMES

It's surprising how easily a child can be transformed into a "P" something. A plastic silver umbrella, a few plastic cameras, some wild sunglasses and you've got a Photographer.

Our Pirate had a plastic eye patch, clip-on gold earring (available in a pack from toy shops), a bandana (any bright scarf will do), cut-off jeans, T-shirt with white shirt tied over it and red gumboots.

The little Princess sported beautiful pink jewellery, a sequinned tiara and a silver staff (we covered a cardboard roll with gold ribbons and glitter) with her pretty gown.

A piece of white felt glued onto a black T-shirt, black leggings, two cardboard and cotton wool ears taped to a plastic headband and some face paint created a gorgeous Panda!

Hair gel and coloured hair spray were the beginnings of our Punk. We cut up an old T-shirt, sprayed it with paint, added some safety pins, teamed it with jeans, sneakers and hot pink glasses. What a transformation!

DECORATIONS

Cut out the appropriate letters from cardboard and crepe paper, spread them all over the house – pinned to walls, hanging from streamers attached to the ceiling, one on the mailbox and a giant letter on the front window.

Flip through magazines and cut out pictures of animals or other things beginning with the party letter. Make a collage of these images (just mount them on a piece of cardboard) or pin them up around the house – if it was an A party you'd have acrobats, artists, apes, ants, Australia, apples and so on.

GAMES

Games should include Pin the Tail on the Pony, Pass the Parcel, Pass the Message and Piggyback Races.

FOOD

The perfectly planned menu could consist of pies, filled baked potatoes, pizza, popcorn or pineapple.

GOODY BAGS

Pack a selection of pencils, pens, pink jelly beans, play dough, pots of paint and paintbrushes, pretzels or peanuts in a pencil case or bundle up cellophane packs of popcorn held at the top with a peg!

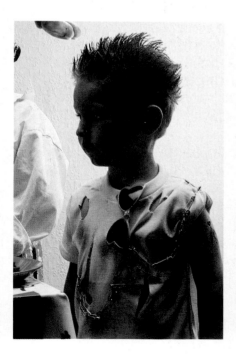

ABOVE: Clockwise from back left: Lovely
Letter Cake, Scrabble Biscuits, Gingerbread
Letters, A,B,C Sandwiches.
Make-up: Johanne Santry. Toys: Toy Buyers Pty Ltd

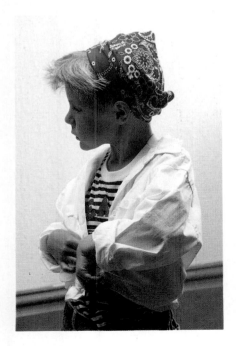

A,B,C SANDWICHES

You may wish to cut all the sandwiches
into the one letter shape in keeping with
the child's first initial. We chose to cut
out several different letters.

2 loaves sliced white and
brown bread

butter for spreading

½ cup ham, finely chopped

½ cup pineapple, finely chopped

1 cup lettuce, shredded

2 hard-boiled eggs, finely chopped

½ cup grated cheese

¼ cup peeled, finely chopped
cucumber

Remove crusts from bread; discard
crusts. Cut bread into letter shapes using
scissors. Lightly butter bread. Make up
sandwiches using suggested fillings.
    Makes about 25.

SCRABBLE BISCUITS

125g butter

½ cup castor sugar

1 egg, beaten

2 cups self-raising flour

1 orange rind, grated

100g dark chocolate

cake sprinkles, various colours

Cream butter and sugar until light and
fluffy, add egg, beat well. Stir in sifted
flour and rind. Mix until well combined.
    Shape balls of mixture into desired
letter shapes. Place onto greased oven
trays, bake in a moderate oven for
about 12 minutes. Allow biscuits to cool
on trays.
    Melt chocolate in saucepan held over
boiling water. Spoon into greaseproof
piping bag. Pipe the letter on the top of
each biscuit following the letter shape.
Top chocolate with cake sprinkles.
Allow chocolate to set before serving.
    Makes about 18.

GINGERBREAD LETTERS

1 teaspoon bicarbonate of soda

2 teaspoons ground ginger

1 teaspoon cinnamon

½ cup brown sugar

2 cups plain flour

1 cup vegetable oil

2 tablespoons golden syrup

1 cup milk

1 egg, beaten

½ quantity glace icing, see glossary

food colouring, various colours

Combine bicarbonate of soda, ginger, cinnamon, sugar and sifted flour in a medium bowl; mix well.

Stir in combined oil, golden syrup, milk and egg; beat until smooth. Pour into greased 23cm square slab pan. Bake in moderate oven for 30 minutes. Cool on a wire rack. Cut gingerbread into small squares.

Tint glace icing desired colours, spoon into greaseproof piping bags. Decorate gingerbread with icing letters.

Makes about 16.

LOVELY LETTER CAKE

2 x 340g packets buttercake mix

1 quantity Vienna cream, see glossary

food colouring, various colours

⅓ cup hundreds and thousands

Make cakes according to directions on packets. Spread mixture into 2 greased 20cm round cake pans. Bake in a moderate oven for about 35 minutes or until firm. Cool on wire rack. Position cakes on prepared board.

Join cakes with a little Vienna cream. Tint ¾ of the cream one colour and spread over sides of cake. Roll sides of cake in hundred and thousands. Spread top of the cake with cream. Tint the remaining cream another colour and spoon into a greased piping bag. Pipe child's initial or appropriate letter onto top of cake.

PERFECTLY PINK PIGLET

1.5m x 115cm-wide pink taffeta

70cm x 115cm-wide pink lining fabric

70cm x 150cm-wide polyester wadding

polyester fibre filling

1m pink satin bias binding

30cm zipper

10cm hook and loop tape

1m narrow elastic

1m blue ribbon

30cm medium-weight wire *or a* wire coat hanger

fusible interfacing scraps

thread

BODY

Make piglet pattern pieces following diagrams. Cut one centre front, two centre backs, four side front/back pieces and two sleeves from taffeta. Cut one 64cm x 5cm tail piece from taffeta. Cut two front/back linings from lining fabric. Cut one centre front, two centre backs and four side/back pieces from wadding. 1cm seam allowance is included.

Tack wadding pieces to the wrong side of corresponding taffeta pieces around edges.

With right sides together, stitch side fronts to centre front. Stitch centre back pieces together below dots, right sides together using 2cm seam allowance. Pin, tack and stitch zipper in back opening.

With right sides together, stitch side backs to centre back. Stitch front to back along shoulder and side seams, right sides

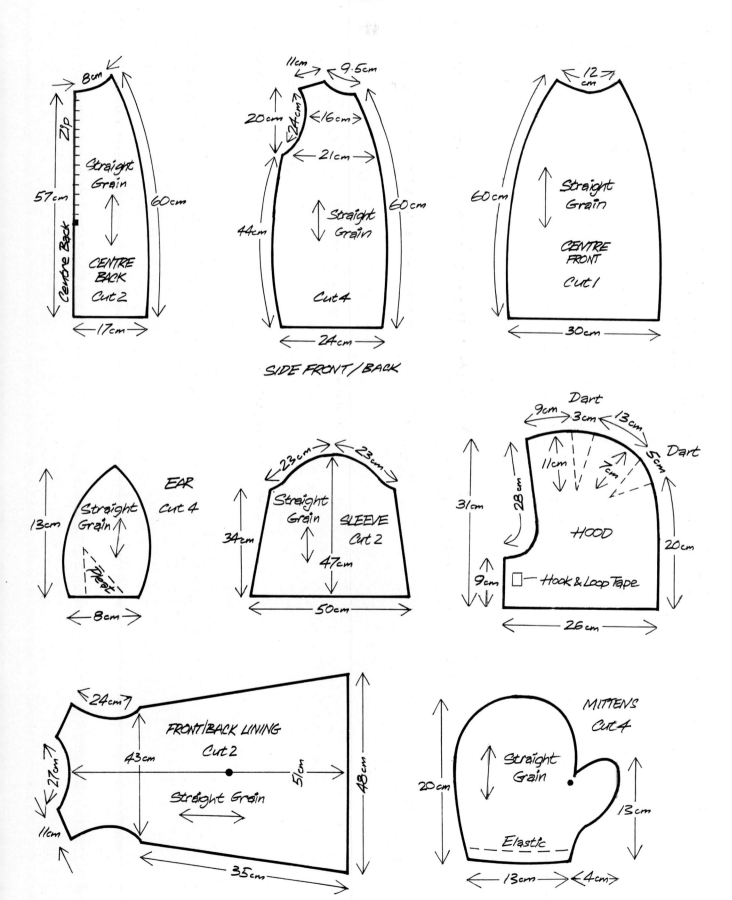

together. Trim and neaten all seams.

Slash back lining piece 30cm from centre back neckline to dot. Turn in and press seam allowance along slashed edge. Work a zigzag bar below slash for reinforcement. Stitch front and back lining pieces together at shoulder and side seams, right sides together. Trim and neaten seams.

Stitch two rows of gathering around lower edge of body section. Turn body section wrong side out. Place lining section inside body section, right sides together. Pull up gathering at lower edge of body to fit lower edge of lining. Pin and stitch lower edges of lining and body sections together. Trim and neaten seam.

Turn lining to inside. Fill gap between lining and body with fibre filling for extra padding, as desired. Tack lining and body together around neck and armhole edges. Handstitch lining to zipper along centre back edges.

With right sides together, stitch sleeve seams. Pin sleeves to body, stitch in place. Trim and neaten seams.

Stitch narrow hems on lower sleeve edges then turn up and stitch 1cm casing leaving small openings for inserting elastic. Cut elastic to fit child's wrists, thread elastic through casings and stitch ends together. Slip-stitch opening closed.

Stitch right side of satin binding to wrong side of neck edge, centring binding so ends form ties at centre back opening. Turn under raw edge of binding, turn

to right side and pin along neckline. Stitch close to edge along length of binding. Knot ends of binding.

Fold tail piece in half lengthways, right sides together, stitch across one end and down one edge. Trim and neaten seam. Turn right side out. Insert wire in tail and handstitch end closed. Twist tail into a corkscrew shape, handstitch in place at centre back just below the zipper. Trim tail with a blue ribbon bow.

MITTENS
Make mitten pattern following diagram. Cut four mitten pieces from taffeta.

Stitch pairs of mittens together around outer edge, right sides together, pivoting needle at dot between thumb and fingers. Clip to dot.

Turn under and stitch a narrow double hem at lower edges. Cut pieces of elastic to fit child's wrists. Position elastic 1.5cm from lower edge on wrong side of fabric. Zigzag in place, stretching elastic to fit and overlapping ends.

HOOD
Make hood and ear patterns following diagram. Cut two hoods from taffeta.

Cut two hoods from lining. Cut four ears from taffeta.

Pin and stitch 2cm-wide darts in hood and hood lining pieces. Press. Stitch taffeta hood pieces together at curved centre seam, right sides together. Trim and neaten seam. Repeat for lining pieces.

Pin hood and lining, right sides together, matching seams and edges. Stitch around edges leaving a 6cm opening in lower back edge. Trim and neaten seam. Turn hood right side out. Slipstitch opening closed, topstitch edges.

Press interfacing to wrong side of two ear pieces. With right sides together stitch remaining ear pieces to interfaced ears, leaving a small opening along bottom edge. Turn ears right side out, slipstitch opening closed. Fold and stitch a pleat in lower edge of each ear as marked on pattern.

Stitch hook and loop tape across chin at point marked on pattern. Fit hood on child's head. Pin ears in position, remove hood, stitch in place. Trim hood with a blue ribbon bow.

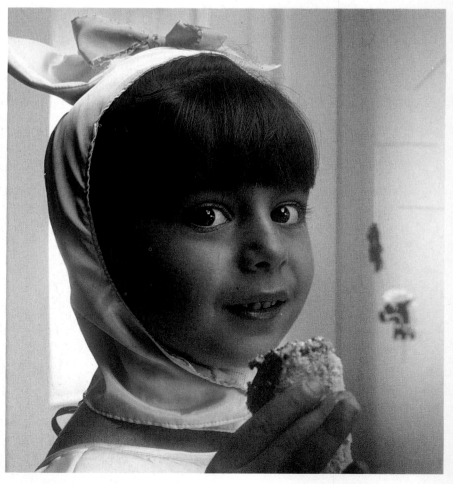

NATURE DISCOVERY

Most children seem to blossom when they're outdoors, in the fresh air, exploring and discovering. Pre-schoolers are fascinated by anything that crawls, wriggles, flies or flutters; these creatures seem to capture their imaginations and keep them engrossed.

Spring and early summer are the best times to capture the life and vitality of your garden – when cicadas, butterflies, birds, dragonflies, crickets and even the odd frog all seem to headline a natural invasion. But if your garden is hardly a showcase of fauna, opt for a local park that's well-endowed with nature's riches ... especially if it has a pond or creek!

Be on the lookout for particularly interesting natural landmarks such as birds' nests, ants' nests, spiders' webs (preferably with a detainee or two!), trails, butterfly or worm cocoons and discarded cicada skins (just about guaranteed to bring squeals of wonder!).

Issue warnings about disturbing any of the study subjects ... especially if they appear to be of the furry and unfriendly variety! It is difficult to impress upon pre-schoolers how important it is not to touch what shouldn't touched, so get together your own team of supervisors – other parents, grandparents or older children.

You might also like to set the team targets – such as finding a snail and its trail, a cocoon and a bird's nest. Accept the fact that while it might be convenient to keep the group ordered and together, children will be children – they'll take off all over the yard to fossick out fascinating finds! One or more guests may fall victim to a sting, graze or bite; do ensure that your first aid kit is close at hand.

INVITATIONS

Send out spider-shaped invitation cards to boys and butterfly cards to girls; or try a snail-shaped or a ladybug card instead! Start with an enticing statement such as:

My garden is full of wonderful things to see, touch, and smell.

Be sure to add details of the time, day, place and theme.

DECORATIONS

Keep them minimal. Perhaps just a brightly coloured cloth on which to spread the party fare.

COSTUMES

Tell the invitees to expect to see some weird and wonderful creatures and ask them to wear comfortable clothes and shoes and a hat – plus sunscreen if it's a mid-summer party. Set aside an hour and a half for the study plus an extra half to one hour for food and other festivities.

If you can rake up some pith helmets, it would add to the theme but otherwise just have extra sunhats on hand and some butterfly nets, plastic magnifying glasses and perhaps a "Bug Catcher" or two (available from toy shops).

GAMES

If anyone has any energy left for games, send everyone off on a Nature Hunt around the house – or garden if they're keen to return – for hidden chocolate frogs; winners get to eat the spoils, of course! But do have more on hand for unsuccessful searchers ... or be prepared for howls of disappointment!

GOODY BAGS

Issue each child with their own "Official Nature Lover" ribbon which they can proudly pin to their chest. And don't forget to pop in a pretty butterfly brooch or tiny ceramic frog amongst the host of confectionery wildlife in the goody bags.

AVOCADO CRAWLIES

3 large ripe avocados, peeled, halved

juice of 2 lemons

1 bunch endive

1 cucumber

6 black olives, pitted, sliced

12 slices brown bread

Remove stones from avocados. Cut in quarters lengthways. Coat each piece of avocado with lemon juice to prevent discolouring. Place avocado pieces on serving plate.

Decorate the top of each piece with endive leaves. Cut cucumber in half, remove seeds. Slice into thick semicircles. Use semicircles to make legs for the avocado crawlie. Place olive slices on avocado crawlie for eyes.

Remove crusts from bread, cut each slice into a leaf shape. Toast, bake or shallow-fry bread until golden and crunchy. Serve around crawlies.

Makes 12.

GARDEN BUGS

12 hard-boiled eggs, peeled

1 cup mashed potato

food colouring, various colours

1 carrot

cloves

alfalfa sprouts

Slice a small piece off one side of eggs to make sure they sit flat on a plate. Tint potato desired colour, spoon into piping bag. Cut carrot into fine 2cm strips. Decorate eggs with piped potato, carrot, cloves and sprouts. The children should not eat the cloves.

Makes 12.

SPIDER SODAS

2 litres chilled cola soft drink

12 scoops vanilla ice-cream

coloured straws

Pour cola into glasses, place 2 scoops of ice-cream into each glass. Serve immediately with straws.

Serves 6.

ABOVE RIGHT: Clockwise from front: Avocado Crawlies, Nature Study Cake, Spider Sodas, Garden Bugs, Sweet Spiders.

SWEET SPIDERS

340g packet buttercake mix

1 quantity Vienna cream, see glossary

brown food colouring

chocolate cake sprinkles

48 Jaffas, approximately

4 licorice straps, cut into thin shreds

24 paper patty cake liners

Make cake according to directions on packet. Place patty cake liners in muffin pans. Fill liners ⅔ full with mixture. Bake in a moderate oven for about 20 minutes or until firm; cool on wire rack.

Tint Vienna cream light brown. Decorate cakes with Vienna cream, chocolate sprinkles, Jaffas and licorice. Chill before serving

Makes about 24.

NATURE STUDY CAKE

2 x 340g packets buttercake mix

1 quantity Vienna cream, see glossary

green food colouring

1 magnifying glass

1 small glass jar

plastic insects

assorted sweets

Make cakes according to directions on packets. Spread mixture into 2 greased 20cm square cake pans. Bake in a moderate oven for about 35 minutes or until firm; cool on wire rack.

Position cakes on prepared board. Join cakes with a little Vienna cream. Tint remaining cream green. Spread cream evenly over sides and top of cake.

Roughen cream with a fork.

Arrange magnifying glass and jar on top of cake. Decorate with plastic insects and sweets.

A sponge rollette cut in half can be positioned on the cake to support jar and lid, if desired.

BRUSH UP

Budding Michaelangelos will jump at the chance to spend a few hours getting messy and "creating" ... and who cares if the resulting scribbles, scrawls and colourful blobs aren't exactly masterpieces – it's the fun that's been had doing it that counts!

Obviously, this is a party for the well-prepared; you'll need to have plenty of space in a room with washable walls and floors – a large kitchen or rumpus room is ideal. Lay down plastic sheeting or several layers of newspaper and try to limit traffic flow through other areas of the house. A patch of lawn or a covered paved area outside are good alternative locations.

To protect cupboards and other inside wall fixtures, stick big sheets across the entire wall area. Another helpful protective ploy is to buy up some oddments of wallpaper and fix them across cupboard and wall faces. At the end of this mess-a-thon, you'll be pleased you invested in a couple of packets of large plastic garbage bags!

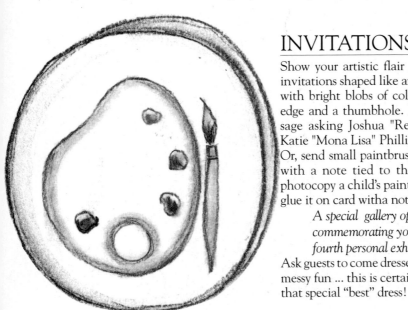

INVITATIONS

Show your artistic flair by sending out invitations shaped like an artist's palette with bright blobs of colour around the edge and a thumbhole. Inscribe a message asking Joshua "Renoir" Wells or Katie "Mona Lisa" Phillips to a paint in. Or, send small paintbrushes in the mail with a note tied to them. You could photocopy a child's painting or drawing, glue it on card with a note to come to:

A special gallery opening commemorating young Claude's fourth personal exhibition!

Ask guests to come dressed for some truly messy fun ... this is certainly no party for that special "best" dress!

DECORATIONS

You'll have little or no need for decoration of any sort ... that would only get in the way of the tiny creative geniuses! Perhaps you could pin some children's painting to the walls – for inspiration! Set out all the materials on a trestle table or benchtop covered with plastic ... you'll need plenty of room and **lots** of materials, as pre-school Picassos can consume arts and crafts resources like there's no tomorrow.

Here's a list of resources and materials you might like to include:

- Old magazines to cut up for collage
- Butcher's paper or large sheets
- Wallpaper oddments
- Fabric, wool and leather scraps
- Old and unwanted greeting cards
- Foil and plastic wrappers
- Crepe paper – strips and balls
- Small twigs and leaves
- Sponges and brushes
- Paint (powdered form is cheaper)
- Crayons and chalks
- Egg cartons and toilet rolls
- Cotton wool and paper doilies
- Play scissors, glue and sticky tape
- Ice-cream containers or flower pots
- Rubber or homemade potato stamps

To avoid paint spillage and mishaps, use shallow trays to hold the paint; cut thin household sponges to fit the paint holes (you can use old patty cake tins or ice cube trays for this) and soak them in paint. Pop sponges into the tray; the children will still be able to soak up lots of paint without using it as a free flowing resource.

Encourage each child to use as many different artistic mediums as possible ... let them stencil, stamp, scribble and scrunch their way to a highly colourful and richly textured work of art. And let's not forget those time-honoured artists assets ... the fingers! Where would pre-schoolers be without fingerpainting? You might like to change things around a little and get your guests to do some toepainting, too!

Enquire at the local pre-school or playgroup of the possibility of borrowing any easels or other painting gear. They may be able to supply you with some inspirational ideas, too. We know of at least one playgroup who offer Mums access to the collection of paint squirter bottles for a small fee or favour.

COSTUMES

Shield the children with inexpensive coveralls made from large plastic garbage bags; simply cut a hole big enough for a head and two for the arms. We made simple smocks from plastic-covered fabric by folding a piece in half, cutting a hole for the child's head and adding motifs cut from coloured contact or tape to the front. If you're lucky, some children may come equipped with their own plastic smock. Some sort of protective headgear is also a good idea, such as an old cap or scarf ... or maybe a beret for that authentic peasant artist image!

We made a genuine artists' cap to heighten the theme, so move over Rembrandt.

GAMES

There's no need for organised games at this party, the young artists will be enthralled for hours painting, drawing, printing and creating!

Art equipment: Teach-em-toys from Pod Australia

GOODY BAGS

Of course, each little artisan gets to take home their masterpieces as well as a goody bag equipped with a small paint box and brush or set of crayons, plus a blank exercise book to encourage them to carry on their artistry at home.

VEGETABLE MURAL

1 loaf sliced white *or* brown bread

butter for spreading

assorted toppings: ham slices, cucumber, carrot, tomatoes, orange slices, asparagus spears, alfalfa sprouts, savoury nibbles

Place bread slices on a large board. Lightly butter each slice. Decorate with toppings to create a picture (the children can help with this one).

SAVOURY BRUSHES AND DIP

1 bunch shallots

1 bunch celery

cherry tomatoes

DIP
2½ cups sour cream

1 packet dry chicken soup mix

red, blue and yellow food colouring

Trim shallots and celery. Using a sharp knife or scissors, fringe one end of each vegetable length. Place in iced water and refrigerate until ends are curly.

DIP: Combine sour cream and soup mix. Separate mixture into three small bowls. Tint each mixture desired colour. Serve dip with shallot and celery curls and cherry tomatoes.

ARTISTS' PALETTES

200g white chocolate

50g dark chocolate

2 teaspoons copha

green, red, yellow and blue food colouring

6 plain rice cakes

Melt chocolate separately in saucepans over boiling water. Stir copha into white chocolate. Tint portions of white chocolate with food colouring. Decorate rice cakes with coloured chocolate and sweets, to resemble an artist's palette.
Makes 6.

LEFT: Vegetable Mural.
ABOVE: Clockwise from front left: Artists' Palettes, Picture Cake, Cakes of Paint, Vegetable Mural, Savoury Brushes and Dip.

PICTURE CAKE

2 x 340g packets chocolate
cake mix

1 quantity Vienna cream, see
glossary

blue, green and brown food
colouring

assorted sweets

licorice

marshmallows

Make cakes according to directions on
packets. Spread mixture into 2 greased
20cm square cake pans. Bake in a
moderate oven for about 35 minutes or
until cakes are firm; cool on wire rack.
Place cakes onto prepared board.

Join cakes with a little Vienna cream.
Tint remaining cream blue for the sky,
green for the grass and brown for the
frame. Spread the sides of the cake with
brown Vienna cream. On the top of the
cake, spread the top half with blue Vienna cream and the bottom with green
Vienna cream. Decorate with remaining
ingredients to create a "painting".

LEFT: Picture Cake.
RIGHT: Red Smock and Turquoise Beret.
FAR RIGHT: Yellow Smock.

CAKES OF PAINT

2 x 340g packets chocolate
cake mix

1 quantity Vienna cream, see
glossary

food colouring, various colours

aluminium foil

paper labels

candy sticks and soft jubes

Make cakes according to directions on
packets. Spread mixture into a greased
20cm x 30cm lamington pan. Bake in
moderate oven for about 40 minutes or
until cakes are firm; cool on a wire rack.

Using the rim of a teacup as a guide,
cut cake into rounds about 8cm wide.
Place cake pieces into freezer for 1 hour
to prevent crumbling.

Tint Vienna cream desired colours.
Decorate cake pieces with Vienna
cream, foil and paper labels to resemble
cans of paint.

Decorate top with coloured candy
sticks, sliced at one end and secured with
a round jube to resemble paint brushes.

RED SMOCK

60cm x 115cm-wide vinyl-coated fabric

1m bias binding

self-adhesive vinyl (we used coloured Contact)

thread

Make the smock pattern following diagram. Cut one smock piece from vinyl fabric. Cut the neck opening and the centre back slit.

Pin and stitch right side of bias binding to wrong side of neck edge, centring binding so ends form ties at centre back opening. Fold binding over to right side of vinyl and stitch close to edge along length of binding. Knot ends of binding.

Cut the desired decorative shapes from the self-adhesive vinyl, peel off the backing and stick shapes in desired positions. Shapes can also be cut from fabric and glued onto the smock, if desired.

YELLOW SMOCK

yellow raincoat

1m bias binding

self-adhesive vinyl (we used coloured Contact)

thread

Cut the collar off the raincoat and decorate in the same way as for Red Smock. The back of the raincoat is used as the front of the smock, so the garment buttons down the back.

TURQUOISE BERET

40cm turquoise velveteen fabric

40cm lining fabric

2m braid

thread

Note. Fits 50cm head.
Make pattern pieces following diagram. Cut one top piece and one underpiece from velveteen. Cut a 54cm x 5cm piece velveteen on bias for band. Cut one top piece and one underpiece from lining. 1cm seam allowance is included.

With right sides together, stitch ends of underpiece together. Press seam open.

Stitch top and underpiece together around outside edge, right sides together. Trim and clip seam. Repeat for lining.

Insert lining in beret and tack pieces together around inside edge of beret.

With right sides together, stitch ends of bias band together. Fold in half, wrong sides together. Press.

With right sides together, stitch one edge of band to inside edge of beret, right sides together and raw edges matching. Trim seam. Press under a narrow hem on the other side of band and turn to inside. Slip-stitch band in place. Press.

Stitch two rows of braid around the edges of the beret and glue or tie braid into a loop or bow for decoration.

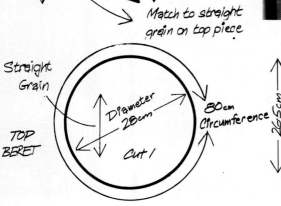

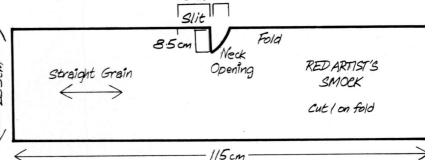

DRAGON'S DEN

When it comes to fun and games and pure flights of fancy, it's hard to beat the romance and fantasy of handsome young knights in shining armour and beautiful damsels in distress. Add the sheer villainy of a fearsome fire-breathing dragon, and you've got the perfect recipe for a child's party that will capture their imaginations and fire their playtime spirit.

And while most pre-schoolers won't be able to grasp the ages-old mysticism of such a caper, they will have a whole barrel of fun playing "goodies and baddies" in and around a majestic cardboard castle!

INVITATIONS

Send out scroll-style invitations, requesting that each damsel and knight attend your family castle, using your surname in the title. For example, Hugo Stewart becomes:

Lord Hugo,
Knight of the Royal Castle Stewart
requests the pleasure of the company of
Lady Susannah, Damsel
of the Castle Smith.

Don't expect your guests to dress up in full costume ... you can make and provide the basics for them.

DECORATIONS

Ideally, the medieval festivities should be located outside, where you can freely construct your cardboard castle without fear of crashing into the light fittings! The idea of the castle is to assemble a dozen or more large cardboard cartons – enquire at local department stores or electrical retailers for suppliers – into a freestanding maze of conjoining "rooms" within a castle. Staples or masking tape can be used to fix boxes in place.

We made our castle from eight large refrigerator boxes, joining them together with tape. We taped down the flaps inside, and cut small holes in the ends and sides of the boxes to allow easy access for energetic lords and ladies. We painted the castle by dabbing on paint with large paintbrushes to cover up brand names and assorted printing. The cardboard flags were stapled to a cardboard cylinder and taped to the castle "wall".

You can paint on or cut out windows (we did the latter) along the sides of boxes. If you're really keen surround the structure with a mock moat, bordered by stiff cardboard and filled with scrunchy, shredded blue and green cellophane.

Alternatively, you might like to use a framework to build the cardboard castle on – such as an existing cubby house, tent, monkey bars set or even your outdoor furniture setting! Try to achieve two or more levels if you do use a solid framework ... it makes for more fun when exploring the various "chambers, tunnels and dungeons" of the castle!

Of course, don't expect your handiwork to stay standing for long ... once your distressed damsels start being rescued by those brave knights, there will be little left but a heap of tangled bodies and cardboard! But imagine the fun they'll have crawling, climbing and more than likely falling, through this magical maze? Add to the pleasure by taping hidden treasures inside the tunnels and turrets ... small parcels of sweets, miniature books and games are ideal unexpected "finds".

If a castle is a little out of your reach, create the feeling of a royal tournament by threading streamers all over the clothes line. Attach balloons and trailing streamers, add a red carpet and some thrones (chairs with gold paper and foil wrapped about them).

COSTUMES

Make up effective cone-style hats with free-flowing crepe, tissue paper or cellophane streamers attached to the top for each attending damsel. Simply roll a sheet of cardboard into a cone, staple or tape at the top and bottom, paint desired colour, tape or staple streamers to peak, staple hat elastic to each side to fit around child's chin and voila, a damsel!

Of course, you must have a shield and sword for each knight. We cut our shields and swords from heavy duty cardboard and painted them gold, silver and majestic red and yellow. We attached a strip of cardboard at the back with tape to make a sturdy handle. You could also cover the "armour" with kitchen foil for that special "shining knight" effect.

GAMES

Perhaps the best part of the day comes when the dragon makes his entrance ... fire-breathing or not, every fairy tale needs a baddie. We made a dragon costume for a child but if this seems too difficult you could try to entice Dad, Big Brother or Uncle to come along as a scary beast. But not too fierce, we don't want to genuinely frighten the party guests! Most children will squeal with delight and run for cover ... coming out to tease the dragon until he finally submits ... to cooking the barbecue swords!
• Finish off the afternoon with a round of Pillow Jousts ... line up two teams to face each other and give each child a cushion or pillow. Now let them knock each other over in a stand up pillow fight! Whoever is left standing is the winner ... but remember, even preschoolers get upset when they lose so make sure there are prizes for all.
• Make a Maypole using a long pole, secured in the ground, with streamers attached to the top. Children take a streamer and thread in and out to create a colourful effect. Littlies may just get tangled up but they will enjoy it anyway.

GOODY BAGS

Take home treats could include bundles of royal "treasure" – wrapped sweets, play jewellery and gold chocolate coins, plus a sword, shield or cone hat.

DELICIOUS DAGGERS

We used licorice allsorts, marshmallows and caramel sweets.

1 punnet strawberries

2 kiwi fruit, peeled

1 rockmelon, peeled

3 bananas, peeled

assorted sweets

Wash and hull strawberries. Cut kiwi fruit, rockmelon and banana into large chunks. Thread fruit and sweets onto bamboo skewers. Cut the sharp ends off the skewers before serving the food to children.
    Makes 6.

DRAGON FOOT PRINTS

24 slices brown and white bread

butter for spreading

6 hard-boiled eggs

green food colouring, optional

¼ cup mayonnaise

salt and pepper

Remove crusts from bread. Place two slices together. Cut into dragon foot shapes using scissors. Lightly butter bread. Peel eggs, mash with a fork. Tint egg green with colouring, if desired. Mix in mayonnaise. Add salt and pepper to taste. Spread egg mixture onto bread.
    Place another cut slice of bread on top of egg mixture.
    Makes 12.

SWEET DAMSELS IN DISTRESS

12 scoops strawberry ice-cream

12 paper patty cake liners

12 sugar ice-cream cones

½ quantity Vienna Cream, see glossary

food colouring, various colours

tulle and lace strips

assorted sweets

Place one scoop of ice-cream into each patty cake liner. Decorate with cones as hats. Use Vienna Cream to attach lace and tulle to cone hats. Create damsel's face with Vienna cream tinted desired colours. Return damsels to freezer until ready to serve.

Makes 12.

SUCCULENT BARBECUED SWORDS

500g chicken fillet

3 onions, quartered

4 zucchini, sliced

2 punnets cherry tomatoes

MARINADE

2 tablespoons soy sauce

2 tablespoons pineapple juice

1 clove garlic, crushed

2 teaspoons honey

Cut chicken into even-sized cubes. Arrange chicken on bamboo skewers with onion, zucchini and tomatoes. Marinate for 1 hour in marinade; drain.

Barbecue or grill until chicken and vegetables are tender.

Cut the sharp ends off the skewers before serving the food to children.

MARINADE: Combine all ingredients together; mix well.

Makes 12.

ICE-CREAM CASTLE CAKE

You will have approximately ½ litre of ice-cream left over from this recipe.

3 x 2 litre cartons strawberry ice-cream

100g cooking chocolate

4 sugar ice-cream cones

licorice pieces

4 small paper flags

Remove ice-cream from one carton (in a block form). Trim edges of ice-cream to form a neat square; place onto prepared board. Using a sharp knife, cut rectangular wedges out of the top of the ice-cream square, to resemble the top of a castle. Place in freezer.

Remove ice-cream from second carton, trim to form a neat square. Cut square evenly into quarters.

Remove castle cake base from freezer. Place a quarter piece of ice-cream at each corner of the main block. Smooth ice-cream with a knife so all joins are concealed. Return cake to freezer.

Remove remaining ice-cream from freezer. Scoop out four large ice-cream balls. Remove cake from freezer. Place one ice-cream scoop on top of each corner block, smoothing joins with a knife. Return cake to freezer and allow to harden.

Melt chocolate over a pan of hot water. Using a pastry brush or spoon, coat each ice-cream cone with melted chocolate. Place onto a foil-lined tray; refrigerate until firm.

Decorate ice-cream castle cake with chocolate-coated cones, licorice and flags prior to serving.

Note. Toothpicks can be used to secure the ice-cream blocks together.

LEFT: Clockwise from back left: Ice-Cream Castle Cake, Sweet Damsels in Distress, Delicious Daggers, Dragon Foot Prints, Succulent Barbecued Swords.

DRAGON COSTUME

3m x 173cm-wide hessian

1.6m x 115cm-wide lining fabric

70cm x 115cm-wide sheer fabric

2 rolls red plastic raffia (available at department and craft stores)

1m bias binding

60cm hook and loop tape

1.2m aluminium stripping (optional, available at hardware stores)

3m tulle

large sequins

polyester wadding

shoe box with lid

masking tape

craft glue

black felt square

orange felt scraps

2 buttons *or* toy eyes

3 polystyrene balls

red paint

coloured cellophane scraps

2.5cm-wide elastic

thread

Make pattern pieces following diagrams. Cut two front body pieces, two back/tail pieces, one undertail, two sleeves and two hoods from hessian. Cut two front body pieces, two backs (cut as marked on pattern), two sleeves and two hoods from lining fabric. 1cm seam allowance is included.

BODY

Cut straw raffia into 17cm lengths and stitch to centre back edge of one back/tail piece. Tie bunches of raffia strands together to give a spiked effect.

Stitch narrow hem along lower edges of back lining pieces. Pin and tack back lining pieces to corresponding edges of back/tail hessian pieces.

With right sides together, stitch back/tail pieces together along centre back seam. Trim and neaten seam.

Apply lining to front and sleeve pieces in the same way as back linings. Pin and stitch shoulder darts in sleeves.

With right sides together, pin and stitch sleeves to fronts and back at

armholes. Trim and neaten seams. Hem lower edges of front sections. Stitch fronts to back at side seams and along underarm seams. Trim and neaten seams.

Hem lower sleeve edges, trim with raffia fringes.

Turn in and hem centre front edges. Apply bias binding to neck edge, centring binding so ends form ties at front. Knot ends of ties. Stitch hook and loop tape on centre front edges for closure.

Using strong thread, stitch aluminium strip to inside of dragon body at waist level to give a round body shape (optional). Glue sequins on body for dragon's scales.

With right sides together, pin and stitch undertail section to tail, matching dots and stitching from dots to tail end. Turn tail right side out, fill tail with tulle. Handstitch top of undertail above dots to wrong side of tail, placing X at centre back seam of tail.

HOOD

Note. The hood can be padded with polyester wadding, if desired. Tack wadding pieces to wrong sides of lining pieces around edges.

Stitch raffia strips to centre seam of one hood piece and lower edges of both hood pieces. With right sides together, stitch hood sections together at centre seam. Stitch hood lining sections in same way.

Stitch hood and hood lining sections together around edges, right sides together, leaving an opening at lower back edge.

Turn hood right side out and handstitch opening closed. Stitch hook and loop tape across chin in position marked on diagram. Tie raffia fringe at back of head into bunches to give a spiked effect.

MASK

Tape lid to shoe box. Cut off one end of box and cut out a section of the bottom, as shown in diagram. Cut a V-shaped section out of the other end to form mouth. Tape edges and corners to reinforce the box.

Glue polyester wadding to top of box to shape forehead, in area marked on diagram.

Cut hessian pieces to cover box and glue in place, turning edges to the inside of box. Cut black felt pieces to fit inside mouth. Place inside mouth and stitch felt to hessian around mouth edges. Cut

a forked tongue from orange felt piece. Glue tongue piece inside mouth.

Glue buttons or toy eyes to two polystyrene balls then glue these on top of head for eyes. Cut the remaining polystyrene ball in half. Paint each half red for nostrils. Cut strips of cellophane and glue to flat sides of nostrils. Glue nostrils, flat side down, on top of head.

Fold sheer fabric piece in half across width. Gather strip across 70cm folded edge and stitch it to the edge of the cut out area on the box bottom (this forms a veil for the mask wearer to look through).

Cut a piece of elastic to fit across cut off box end (this elastic will hold the mask on the child's head). Fit mask on child and adjust elastic, remove mask and stitch elastic in place. Stitch a second piece of elastic from top of mask to first elastic strip as shown in diagram.

MITTENS

Make pattern following diagrams and instructions for Piglet Mittens on page 45 and 46. Make as for Piglet Mittens.

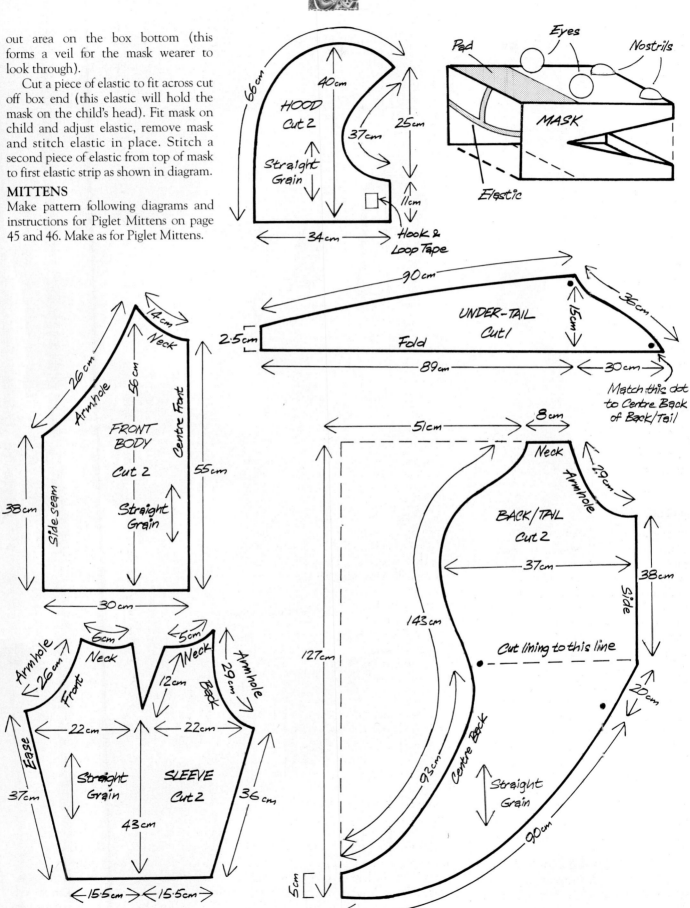

6 TO 8 YEARS

Children aged from 6 to 8 years are always thrilled by the prospect of a party. Generally they can play without much supervision and many parents find it a good idea to allocate some free time during the party for unstructured play in the backyard (if you have one). If you are planning to have a large number of children present you may find it easier to hold the party somewhere where there is space for them to run around – a park or a community hall.

✳ As these children have all started school, they generally respond well to instructions, although you shouldn't presume that they can all read well, even if your own child is quite adept at it. Any written instructions associated with games should be given out when an adult is present so they can step in if the child is having difficulty understanding the instructions.

✳ Some children aged from 6 to 8 often prefer to only have children of their own sex at their parties. If you have both sexes you may find that they tend to separate into two groups anyway. Keeping it to one sex also helps to keep the numbers down. One adult to five children is a good mix at this age and we wouldn't recommend any more than 12 children unless you have a lot of help and a lot of space.

✳ Keep it short and simple! We recommend about three hours as a maximum for a party, two if you have a limited space.

✳ Children of this age are often very conservative when it comes to food. They like to be familiar with what is on the table before they try it. Use your child as a guide – don't put hours of effort into fancy party food when you know your own child prefers cocktail frankfurts. If the food is simple, enliven it with whacky names – such as "devilled dinosaur bones" for simple barbecued chops or "magnetic moon rocks" for chocolate crackles.

✳ While we have recommended games that suit each theme, don't be afraid to use the tried and true party games such as Pass the Parcel, Hide and Seek, Pin the Tail on the Donkey etc. Children at this age like to know the rules and often feel disappointed if these old favourites are not included. Try and ensure that each child receives some sort of prize. You may find it easier to buy lots of smaller prizes rather than one or two bigger ones. It will save a lot of tears in the long run.

✳ Don't forget some sort of goody bag for the children to take home with them. You will find it easier if you hide them until the children are walking out the door. Include some "healthy" foods in the bags too – dried apricots or apples, packets of sultanas, an apple or cheese stick.

RED, WHITE AND BLUE

In these days of American sit-coms and movies, almost all children of this age group are familiar with American food and family life.

INVITATIONS

Invitations could feature a Stars and Stripes theme – draw an American flag on the card or cut cards into flag shapes. Perhaps send out invitations in the shape of a hamburger or hot dog (with stars and stripes floating on it?). Another idea is to send out your daughter or son dressed as an American Gridiron player and hand-deliver invitations shaped like a football.

DECORATIONS

Continue the Stars and Stripes idea; streamers in red, white and blue will add to the atmosphere, while some simple white cardboard stars scattered throughout the house (hung from the ceiling or stuck onto doors or walls) will also help to set the scene. You may also like to get your children to cut up some old magazines and stick pictures of hamburgers, hot dogs or apple pies around the room. If you're having the party in a hall and you want to liven it up a little, borrow a flag from a theatre hire shop or make your own using fabric paint.

COSTUMES

We made the most of fluoro colours and roller skates and created a Venice Beach girl. A Cheerleader was achieved with pompoms, shorts and T-shirt. A plaited headdress and feather, jeans and zinc cream used as face paint made our Red Indian. And, the Gridiron player simply wore a black t-shirt and track pants with a helmet.

You could suggest that the children come dressed in all red, white and blue, as baseball players or an American folk hero such as Davy Crockett – all they really need is the right hat!

Our Cowboy costume is simple – just a hat, checked shirt and bolero (shop bought). His horse will take a bit of time to make, but it's well worth the effort.

LEFT: Clockwise from right: Mini Hot Dogs with Ketchup, Burger and Fries, Flying the Flag Cake, Muppet Cakes.
Table and chairs: Cotswold Garden Furniture

BURGER AND FRIES

6 beef burgers

½ cup shredded lettuce

½ cup mayonnaise

2 tomatoes, sliced

3 gherkins, sliced

tomato sauce

6 fresh hamburger buns

500g frozen french fries

oil for deep-frying

Cook beef burgers as directed on packet. Place on warm hamburger buns with mayonnaise, lettuce, tomato, gherkin and sauce. Deep-fry french fries in hot oil until golden, drain. Serve burger and fries hot.

Serves 6.

MINI HOTDOGS WITH KETCHUP

2 sheets ready rolled puff pastry

1 egg, beaten

16 cocktail frankfurts

1 tablespoon sesame seeds

Allow pastry sheets to thaw to room temperature. Cut each sheet into 8 even squares. Brush with beaten egg. Place a frankfurt diagonally across each pastry square. Wrap two opposite points of pastry around frankfurt. Brush with egg lightly and sprinkle with sesame seeds. Bake in a moderately hot oven for 12-15 minutes or until golden.

Serve with a big bowl of tomato sauce (ketchup) for dipping.

Makes 16.

SHAKES

1½ litres cold milk

6 scoops chocolate ice-cream

6 tablespoons chocolate topping

whipped cream

grated chocolate

Combine milk, ice-cream and topping in a food processor or blender. Process until frothy. Pour into tall cups or glasses. Decorate each shake with whipped cream and chocolate.

Serves about 6.

GAMES

● Borrow the Halloween idea of Bobbing for Apples. Fill tubs or dishes with water and apples and let the children bend over the tub and try to grab the apples with their teeth. We suggest you keep plenty of towels handy and use an outside location, or else cover the floor with plastic or towels.!

● A game of Baseball can be easy to organise if you have some space in the backyard. Go easy on the rules and try and make sure each child gets a bat. Be flexible about the success of a structured game like baseball. Most parents find it easier to be prepared to either spend a couple of hours on the game or abandon it after 15 minutes.

● Doughnut Munching: Tie doughnuts to a clothes-line or similar, using lengths of string or ribbon. Watch the fun as children, with hands behind their backs, try to catch a yummy doughnut in their mouth.

● Musical Hats: Stand children in a circle, all facing the same way. Make sure each child is wearing a hat (have baseball caps, cowboys hats, Indian feathers or marine caps on hand). When the music starts children take the hat from the child in front. The one without a hat when the music stops, sits out the game. Take another hat out and restart the music.

GOODY BAGS

Small toy basketballs or baseballs are a good idea for both sexes. Boys and girls will like baseball caps, which often can be bought quite cheaply at a large chain store. Give every child a cap instead of a party hat as they come through the door. And, don't forget the bubblegum – in the goody bags for later!

OTHER THEMES

You could try a French Party – same red, white and blue theme, serve croissants, French sticks and pastries; or a Fijian Party where everyone has to wear tropical shirts, grass skirts and leis. Food could include tropical fruits and punches, seafood kebabs and baked potatoes.

Or, deck the house in red, white and green, serve pizzas and pasta, buy soccer balls for games and call it an Italian Party. There are lots of country themes – Britain, Australia, China or Greece to name but a few.

MUPPET CAKES

340g packet buttercake mix

24 paper patty cake liners

1 quantity Vienna cream, see glossary

food colouring, various colours

variety of sweets

Make cake according to directions on packet. Place patty cake liners in muffin pans. Two-thirds fill patty cake liners with mixture, bake in a moderate oven for about 20 minutes or until firm; cool on a wire rack. Tint Vienna cream in desired colours. Decorate cakes with Vienna cream and sweets to resemble your child's favourite Muppet stars; we created Miss Piggy, Kermit, Fozie Bear and Gonzo.

Makes 24.

FAR LEFT, TOP: Doughnut Munching.
FAR LEFT, BOTTOM: Apple Bobbing.
LEFT: Muppet Cake.
ABOVE: Flying the Flag Cake.
Apple bobbing tub: Woollahra Galleries Antiques

FLYING THE FLAG CAKE

3 x 340g packets buttercake mix

2 quantities Vienna cream, see glossary

blue and red food colouring

100g white chocolate

Make cakes according to directions on packets. Spread mixture into 2 greased 20cm x 30cm lamington pans. Bake in a moderate oven for about 40 minutes or until firm; cool on wire racks. Place on prepared board. Join cakes with a little Vienna cream. Tint ¼ of Vienna cream royal blue and ¼ bright red, leave remaining ½ of cream white.

Outline a square in top left-hand corner of cake, fill in with blue cream. Spread red and white cream in alternating stripes across top and sides of cake.

Melt chocolate over pan of hot water, spoon into greaseproof piping bag. Pipe small stars onto a foil-lined tray, refrigerate until hard. Remove from tray and place on blue section of cake.

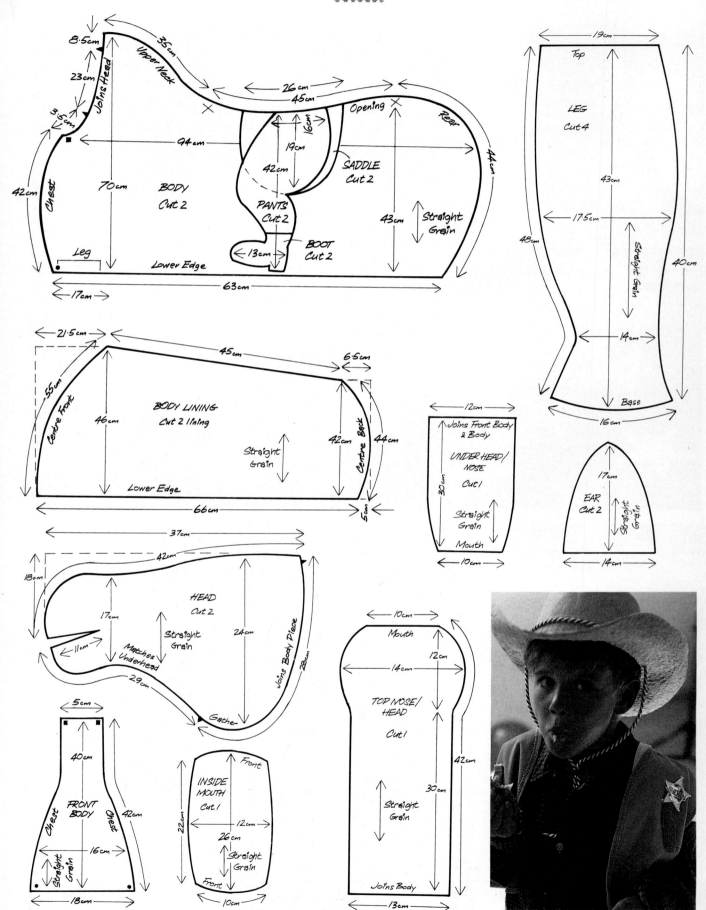

LEG
Cut 4

19cm · Top · 43cm · Straight Grain · 17·5cm · 14cm · 40cm · 45cm · 16cm · Base

BODY
Cut 2

8·5cm · Upper Neck · 35cm · 23cm · Joins Head · 3·5cm · Chest · 42cm · 70cm · 94cm · 26cm · 45cm · Opening · 16cm · 19cm · 42cm · SADDLE Cut 2 · Rear · 44cm · PANTS Cut 2 · BOOT Cut 2 · 13cm · 43cm · Straight Grain · Leg · Lower Edge · 17cm · 63cm

BODY LINING
Cut 2 lining

21·5cm · Centre Front · 55cm · 45cm · 6·5cm · 46cm · Straight Grain · 42cm · Centre Back · 44cm · Lower Edge · 66cm · 5cm

UNDER HEAD/NOSE
Cut 1

12cm · Joins Front Body & Body · 30cm · Straight Grain · Mouth · 10cm

EAR
Cut 2

17cm · Straight Grain · 14cm

HEAD
Cut 2

18cm · 37cm · 42cm · 17cm · Straight Grain · 24cm · Joins Body Piece · 23cm · 11cm · Matches Underhead · 29cm · Gather

TOP NOSE/HEAD
Cut 1

10cm · Mouth · 12cm · 14cm · 42cm · 30cm · Straight Grain · Joins Body · 13cm

FRONT BODY

5cm · 40cm · Chest · 42cm · Chest · Straight Grain · 16cm · 18cm

INSIDE MOUTH
Cut 1

Front · 22cm · 12cm · 26cm · Straight Grain · Front · 10cm

COWBOY AND HORSE

2.5m x 150cm-wide fur fabric

30cm x 115cm-wide suede fabric

1m x 115cm-wide lining fabric

20cm vinyl fabric

small scrap pink fabric

2 red felt squares

cardboard

craft glue

fringing

small scraps of black felt

polyester fibre filling (enough to fill entire horse)

5.2m ribbon

thick wool

four metal rings

large plastic eyes

small scrap of thin white foam

thread

Make horse pattern pieces following diagrams. Cut two pants from suede. Cut two bodies, two heads, four legs, two ears, one under nose/head and one top nose/head from fur fabric. Cut two body linings and two ears from lining fabric. Cut one inside mouth from pink fabric and one from cardboard. Cut two saddles from vinyl. Cut two boots from red felt. 1cm seam allowance is included.

HORSE

With right sides together, stitch lining to ears leaving 5cm openings at lower edges. Trim and neaten seams. Turn right side out and handstitch openings closed. Fold ears in half lengthways, lining sides together, stitch lower edges together.

Stitch 42cm edges of heads to long edges of top nose/head piece. Trim and neaten seams. Stitch under nose/head between dot and notch on lower edges of heads. Trim and neaten seams.

With right sides together, stitch inside mouth fabric to mouth opening in head, clipping seams at points. Trim and neaten seams. Turn right side out, fold cardboard inside mouth in half and glue in place, in mouth, to stiffen. Firmly fill head with fibre filling. Cut a red felt tongue. Glue tongue to inside mouth.

With right sides together stitch pairs of legs together along sides and base.

Trim and neaten seams, turn to right side and insert filling. Cut black felt in shape of hooves, glue to front of foot.

Pin and stitch body pieces to front body piece along chest edge matching dots and squares, neaten seams. With right sides together, stitch body pieces together along upper edge and rear, leaving opening at upper edge between Xs. Pin and stitch legs in position on lower edge of body.

Gather head, between notches, at curve around jawline. With right sides together, stitch head to body, matching notches. Trim, neaten and clip seams.

With right sides together, stitch lining pieces together at centre front and centre back. With right sides together, pin and stitch lower edge of lining to lower edge of body, with legs between lining and body, and gathering body to fit lining. Trim and neaten seam. Turn lining to inside body, turn top edge seam

allowances of body and lining to wrong side. Pin and stitch top edges of lining and body together between Xs, leaving a 20cm opening.

Insert filling in neck and body. Hand-stitch opening closed.

Glue saddle pieces to body as marked on diagram. Glue pants over saddle. Glue boots to ends of pants and trim with fringing. Cut 50cm strands of wool and glue or stitch centres of strands to neck to form mane. Repeat to form tail using longer strands of wool.

Stitch ears to head. Cut pieces of ribbon and stitch or glue to metal rings and to horse head to form reins. Cut pieces of black felt for eyes. Glue to head and glue plastic eyes on top. Cut two teeth from foam and glue to top of mouth.

Cut a 2m piece of ribbon in half and stitch lengths to front of lining on both sides. Tie these around child's waist when costume is being worn.

OVER THE RAINBOW

Children are always fascinated by rainbows whether it be the myriad of colours or the elusive pot of gold at the end that captures their attention! The spectrum of colours makes your job easy – there are lots of possibilities for decorations, costumes and prizes.

INVITATIONS

A simple rainbow shape, cut out of card and coloured in by your child, a pot of gold (pot-shaped and painted gold) or perhaps you may like to tie cards around bunches of tiny balloons and hand deliver them.

DECORATIONS

Use lots of pretty streamers around the room and clusters of coloured balloons. You may like to try to get the party guests to make their own party hats with pastel crayons or pencils and a smattering of coloured glitter. (If you do this make sure the floor and walls are covered to prevent nasty decorating surprises!)

BELOW: Clockwise from centre front: Rainbow Ribbon Sandwiches, Goody Bags, Harlequin Biscuits, Rainbow Cake, Pots of Gold.

All plastic plates, cups, bowls: Decor Corporation. Table and chairs: Cotswold Garden Furniture

Come to a Rainbow Party Mary + find gold!
Date: 7th Jan.   Time: 10am
Place: 6 Dudley St. Rosemont.

COSTUMES

Encourage the guests to dress in bright colours or come as a green Leprechaun (he guards the pot of gold).

We made a simple skirt and top sewed in multi-coloured panels and a layered tulle skirt with matching accessories.

GAMES

- A Treasure Hunt is the ideal game for this party. Hide a few pots of gold (sweets wrapped in gold paper) around a selected room and let the children scramble for as many sweets they can find. This ensures that everyone wins a little. Keep a couple of sweets in reserve in case some children don't find any.
- Try a variation of Pass the Parcel with each layer wrapped in different coloured paper and the prize wrapped in gold.
- Pot of Gold: Place a clothes basket or bucket about 3 metres away from the line where children will stand. Give each child about three items to throw into the basket (soft toys, plastic balls). Each child to get a hole in one can select from the pot of gold – either gold foil-covered chocolate coins or assorted treats.
- Rainbow Messages: Choose a selection of rainbow coloured pieces of paper. Write a message on each slip, wrap up tightly and pop inside a deflated balloon. Each child has to blow up, then burst their balloon (no pins allowed) and perform the task inside eg. hop on one foot five times, turn around three times, sing Twinkle Twinkle Little Star, kiss the person next to them. Each child that completes their task gets a prize. Keep the tasks simple so that each child can get a reward.
- Wheelbarrow Race to the Rainbow's End: Set up an archway or two poles of colourful streamers in the garden or rumpus room. Pairs of children must race to the rainbow's end, one holding the other's legs up when they "run" on their hands. The winners get the pot of gold – a large paper basket of sweets or two lots of coloured pencils, pastels or felt-tipped pens and erasers.

GOODY BAGS

Any prizes that are gold coloured are sure to be popular. Try those small bags filled with chocolates shaped like golden money. Wrap up sweets in gold (yellow) coloured cellophane. Don't forget to include rainbow balls (those hard round sweets that change colour as children suck them) in the sweets bag.

RAINBOW RIBBON SANDWICHES

6 slices brown bread

6 slices white bread

6 slices wholemeal bread

butter for spreading

250g soft cream cheese

mauve and blue colourings

2 carrots, grated

1 cup shredded lettuce

250g can red salmon, drained

Butter bread lightly, place brown bread out on board. Divide cream cheese in half, tint half mauve and the remaining half blue. Alternately spread onto bread. Top with grated carrot, white bread slices, shredded lettuce, salmon and wholemeal bread slices. Cut crusts from sandwiches with a serrated edged knife. Slice each sandwich into 3 lengths. Serve ribbon sandwiches cut side up.
  Makes 18.

HARLEQUIN BISCUITS

1 cup brown sugar

125g butter

1 egg, beaten

1 teaspoon vanilla essence

1½ cups plain flour

½ teaspoon baking powder

250g clear, coloured, hard sweets

Cream sugar and butter together until light and fluffy. Add egg and essence, mix well. Fold in sifted flour and baking powder. Wrap and chill biscuit dough 20 minutes in the refrigerator.

Separate sweets into colours, crush each colour individually in a plastic bag with a rolling pin or metal mallet.

Roll biscuit mixture into thin logs on a floured surface. Arrange in rainbow shapes on foil-lined oven trays. Bake in a moderate oven for 5 minutes, remove from oven. Place crushed sweets between sections of dough to form rainbows. Return to oven, bake a further 10 minutes or until golden. Cool on foil-lined trays for 30 minutes.

Makes about 6-8.

POTS OF GOLD

1 cup sugar

¾ cup water

2 teaspoons honey

1 ½ cups Honey Smacks

12 foil patty cake liners

yellow jelly beans

gold chocolate coins

Place sugar and water into heavy-based saucepan. Heat, stirring gently, until sugar dissolves, simmer until golden, remove from heat, stand 3 minutes. Quickly stir in honey and Honey Smacks. Using an oiled metal spoon, spoon into foil cake liners. Decorate with jelly beans and chocolate coins.

Makes about 12.

ABOVE FAR LEFT: Pot of Gold.
BELOW LEFT: Rainbow Messages.
ABOVE: From top: Harlequin Biscuits, Pots of Gold.

RAINBOW CAKE

2 x 340g packets buttercake mix

1 quantity Vienna cream, see glossary

red, blue, yellow, mauve, green and orange food colourings

Make cakes according to directions on packets. Spread into a greased 28cm cake pan. Bake in a moderate oven for 50 minutes or until firm; cool on a wire rack. Cut cake in half to form two semi-circles, join with a little Vienna cream. Place on prepared board, cut side down.

Divide Vienna cream into six even portions, tint with food colourings. Spoon into piping bag.

Pipe Vienna cream onto front of cake to resemble a rainbow. Smooth each colour with an oiled knife. Repeat for back of cake, or cover back and top of cake one colour only.

RAINBOW MAGIC

4 pieces 1.7m x 140cm-wide tulle, in different colours

4cm-wide elastic (length to fit child's waist)

3m wire or cane, for stiffening edge of skirt

4 pieces 4m-long bias binding, in different colours

6 pieces 1.6m-long ribbon, in different colours

small piece lightweight wire

2 pairs cotton tights, in different colours

1m coloured braid

Make skirt pattern following diagram and adjust to desired length. (The longest layer of our skirt was 60cm.) Cut 8 pieces tulle (4 skirt layers), each layer a different colour. 1cm seam allowance is included.

Stitch corresponding tulle pieces together at side seams to make four skirt layers. Place four skirt layers together and trim top three layers so each one is 7cm shorter than the previous one (shortest layer on top).

Separate skirt layers. Mark positions for contrast strips on top layer as marked on pattern. Cut three contrasting coloured tulle pieces to fit marked sections. Pin and stitch contrast pieces in position on right side of back skirt.

Bind hem of bottom three skirt layers with contrasting bias binding. Stitch binding down each side seam of shortest skirt layer, leaving an opening at each end, to make casing for wire or cane. Bind front edge of top skirt layer with bias binding. Stitch binding to back skirt edge leaving openings at each end to make casing.

Tack all skirt layers together at waist placing shortest layer on top. Bind waist edges together with bias binding.

Measure child's waist, cut elastic to fit and stitch ends of elastic together for waistband. Divide elastic band into quarters and mark each with a pin. Mark quarters of skirt waist with pins. Stitch elastic to skirt, matching pins and stretching elastic as you stitch.

Insert wire or cane into back of top skirt layer along hem edge casing. Insert separate pieces into side seams through casing. Knot 1m lengths of ribbon together halfway along their length, stitch to waist at front.

TOP, TIGHTS AND SLEEVES
Cut each pair of tights into halves along centre seam. Stitch two contrasting coloured legs together to make a two-tone pair of tights.

Cut the tops off the remaining tights legs to form 20cm long pieces. Stitch 20cm sections together, right sides facing, to form a tube top. Neaten the lower edge. Stitch 60cm lengths of ribbon to top to form halter strap.

The remaining legs of the tights are worn as sleeves. Trim to correct length, neaten raw edges, cut pieces of braid and tie around upper edges to hold in place. A tuck may need to be stitched in the lower edge so sleeves fit.

HEADBAND
Bend lightweight wire into an arc to form headband base. Twist one end of wire into a small loop. Cut four or five 50cm x 12cm strips of contrasting coloured tulle. Fold each tulle strip in half and thread onto wire headband base. Twist other end of wire into a loop. Cut narrow elastic to fit around base of child's head. Tie one end of elastic onto one looped end of wire. Adjust elastic to fit child's head and tie to other wire loop.

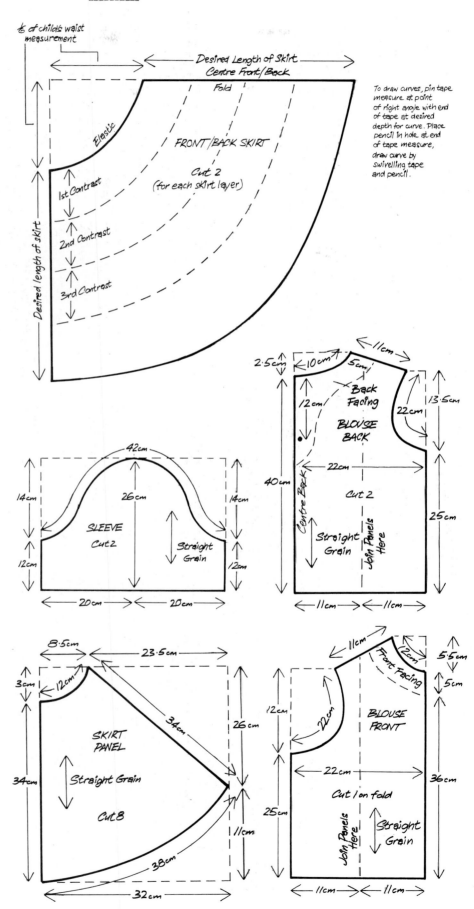

SPECTRUM SUIT

2 pieces 80cm x 115cm-wide fabric, in different colours

4 pieces 40cm x 115cm-wide fabric, in different colours

fishing line

small button

12mm-wide elastic (length to fit child's waist)

1m x 5mm-wide elastic

Make pattern following diagram. Cut eight skirt panels (we cut two panels from each of the larger quantities of coloured fabrics and one from each of the other four fabrics). Cut front and back pattern pieces along dotted line from shoulder to lower edge. Cut eight contrasting coloured panels for front and back of top adding 1cm seam allowance at the cut edge of pattern (along dotted line). (We cut panels to correspond with colours in skirt). Cut two different coloured sleeves. Cut one front and two back facings for top as marked on pattern. 1cm seam allowance is included.

With right sides together, stitch skirt panels together. Trim and neaten seams. Turn under a narrow hem along the top edge. Stitch 12mm-wide elastic together at ends. Divide elastic into quarters and mark quarters with pins. Divide and mark skirt quarters in same way. Stitch elastic to wrong side of skirt stretching elastic as you sew.

Cut a piece of fishing line slightly longer than the hem circumference. Turn up and stitch hem, zigzagging over fishing line and stretching fabric as you sew. Trim fishing line.

Join coloured panels for blouse front. Join panels for back, stitching below dot at centre back. Stitch front to back, right sides together, at shoulder and side seams. Stitch front facing and back facings together at shoulder seams. Stitch lower section of back facings together at centre back seam below dot. Turn up and stitch a narrow hem along lower edge of facing.

With right sides together, stitch facing to blouse matching shoulder seams and stitching around centre back opening (above dot). Trim, clip and neaten seam. Hem lower edge of blouse. Attach button to centre back neck opening, make loop to correspond.

With right sides together, stitch sleeves along underarm seams. Hem lower edge of sleeves using fishing line in the same way as skirt hem. Cut 2 pieces 5mm-wide elastic to fit around child's arms. Stitch elastic around sleeve, positioning it 5cm above lower edge, stretching elastic as you sew.

Pin and stitch sleeves to blouse, right sides together. Trim and neaten seams.

Cut two 85cm x 17cm strips fabric from large fabric quantities. Stitch strips right sides together at ends, to form a waist sash. Stitch a narrow hem around all edges.

ROLL UP, ROLL UP

The lure of the big top filled with dazzling acrobats, fierce lions and magical clowns is irresistible to children. So create a circus party at home with a generous sprinkling of balloons, plus a parade of fun food and pint-sized performers in clever costumes.

INVITATIONS

Cut two pieces of cardboard in the shape of a circus tent. Colour the front with stripes. Cut a large flap in the front which can be folded back. Stick the front piece onto the other piece of cardboard, open the flap, write the party details underneath. Or, wrap a bright red plastic clown's nose around a piece of strong cardboard, write the details on the front.

DECORATIONS

Lots of brightly coloured balloons add to the circus atmosphere. Hang balloons from the ceiling, from doors and perhaps even put a collection of balloons at the front door as a welcome. A big piece of fabric (ours was crushed velvet) draped across the wall gives the feeling of a tent. We also covered the floor with fabric.

You are invited to a Circus Party Tom!
Date: 10th July   Time: 11a.m   Place: 12
Jeffreys Avenue Park-Side.   BYO NOSE!

All plastic plates, cups: Decor Corporation. Table and chairs: Cotswold Garden Furniture. Make-up: Johanne Santry

COSTUMES

We kept the costumes fairly simple. Our Strongman had a moustache painted on and wore an old bathing costume backwards! The Tightrope-walker wore a leotard, tights and ballerina points, the Bellydancer wore a sheer tunic with gold coins sewn on to it. We used a man's shirt for the boy's Clown suit and painted his face to look like a chequerboard!

The Trapeze Artist's costume features leggings, a sequined top and a satin cape, while the Lion is an all-in-one body suit with a separate head.

The adult Clown's costume is an old pair of white overalls artistically dabbed and sprayed with colourful paint.

GAMES

● Children of this age may enjoy Tightrope Walking! Of course, to keep it safe you may like to lay a piece of string or wooden plank on the ground. Every child who makes it to the other end without falling gets a prize.

● If funds permit, hire a clown for the occasion. Clowns are often easy to find – ask around for a good one or go through the Yellow Pages. If you wish, you can ask for references from previous children's parties and ring up the parents for their opinions.

● Face Painting: Buy some face paint and set up a "Performers' Corner", draped with fabric and featuring a mirror or two. Get a willing neighbour or relative in to paint the children's faces – tigers, happy and sad clowns, zebras, giraffes and so on. It helps if the painter has an artistic

streak but if not, make sure there's lots of pictures handy for reference.

● Pin the Tail on the Lion. Draw a large lion. Place a cross where the tail should be. Make a tail from yellow cord with a tassel at one end and a drawing pin at the other. Blindfold each child and give them the lion's "tail". The child who places the tail closest to the cross wins.

GOODY BAGS

Funny masks with big red noses would be a great prize! Other ideas include plastic or rubber circus animals – bears, lions, monkeys, small books about animals, or rubber stamps of animals. Add a packet of fairy floss or a gleaming toffee apple and a packet of face paint. Wrap up the goodies in striped or satin fabric.

PARTY CLOWNS

12 scoops ice-cream

12 paper patty cake liners

12 sugar ice-cream cones

glace cherries

licorice pieces

1 quantity Vienna cream, see glossary

food colouring, various colours

Place ice-cream into patty cake liners. Place a cone on top of each. Decorate with cherries and licorice to resemble clown faces.

Tint Vienna cream desired bright colours. Spoon into a piping bag, decorate clown hats with Vienna cream. Return to freezer.

Makes 12.

CHOCOLATE MONKEYS

250g dark chocolate

6 bananas

sliced almond flakes

white marshmallows

Melt chocolate in saucepan over hot water. Slice bananas in half crossways, About 3cm from each cut edge, cut completely through skin (not banana) all the way around. Peel skin away from top of banana, stopping at scored line, leaving skin on at base so that a child can easily hold the banana. Insert two almonds on each side at top of banana to look like ears. Dip ends of bananas in chocolate, allowing chocolate to drip over the peel. Place in refrigerator to set slightly. Decorate with marshmallows to resemble monkeys' faces. Stand in freezer until firm.

Makes 12.

ABOVE: From left: Party Clowns, Merry-Go-Round Cake, Tamed Animals.
ABOVE RIGHT: Chocolate Monkeys.
LEFT: Tightrope Walking.
FAR LEFT: Pin the Tail on the Lion.

TAMED ANIMALS

12 scoops mashed potato

2½ cups dry breadcrumbs

oil for deep-frying

potato crisps

sliced black olives

assorted vegetable slices: carrot, celery, shallot

corn chips

Roll potato in breadcrumbs. Deep-fry in hot oil until golden, drain potatoes on absorbent paper.

Decorate each potato ball with remaining ingredients to resemble lions, tigers, elephants and monkeys.

Makes 12.

MERRY-GO-ROUND CAKE

2 x 340g packets chocolate cake mix

1 quantity Vienna cream, see glossary

1 tablespoon cocoa

brown food colouring

2 cups grated dark chocolate

candy sticks

small plastic toys

ribbons

Make cakes according to directions on packets. Spread mixture into 2 greased 20cm round cake pans. Bake in a moderate oven for about 35 minutes or until firm; cool on wire racks.

Join cakes with a little Vienna cream. Stir sifted cocoa into remaining cream, add colouring to make brown. Spread cream over cake. Coat cake sides with grated chocolate, sprinkle with remaining chocolate on top. Place cake on prepared board. Decorate cake with candy sticks, toys and ribbons, to resemble a merry-go-round.

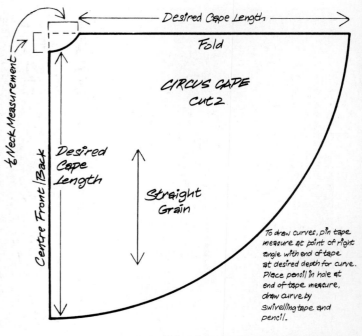

Desired Cape Length

Fold

CIRCUS CAPE
Cut 2

½ Neck Measurement

Centre Front/Back

Desired Cape Length

Straight Grain

To draw curves, pin tape measure at point of right angle with end of tape at desired depth for curve. Place pencil in hole at end of tape measure, draw curve by swivelling tape and pencil.

TRAPEZE COSTUME

4.6m x 115cm-wide satin fabric

bias binding

short feather boa

metallic or brightly coloured fabric scraps

tracing paper

1m ribbon

glitter fabric pen

50cm x 30cm-wide stretch sequined fabric (or amount to fit child's chest measurement)

2m sequined cord

purchased footless cotton tights

thread

Make pattern piece following diagram. Cut two cape pieces from satin fabric. (Our cape was 100cm long.) 1cm seam allowance is included.

CAPE

With right sides together, stitch cape pieces along centre back seam. Trim and neaten seam.

Turn in and stitch a narrow hem at lower edge. Turn in and stitch 1.5cm hems along centre front edges. Apply bias binding to neck edge. Cut feather boa to fit neck edge and glue or hand-stitch in place.

Draw star and lightning shapes on tracing paper and transfer outlines to metallic or brightly coloured fabric. Cut out applique shapes, pin on cape. Stitch around shapes using close zigzag.

Cut ribbon in half and stitch a piece to each side of front neck edge. Decorate cape with glitter pen.

TOP

Stitch ends of sequined fabric together to form a tube. Trim and neaten seam. (Seam sits at the centre back.)

Fit the top and cut sequined cord into two pieces to form straps. Stitch straps in place on upper edge of top.

TIGHTS

Decorate tights with glitter pen.

LOUIE THE LION

2m x 150cm-wide fur fabric

thick wool, for mane

polyester fibre filling

1m x 10mm-wide elastic

40cm x 5mm-wide elastic

35cm hook and loop tape

scraps of white felt

large plastic eyes

plastic nose

craft glue

black pipe-cleaners

65cm cotton tape

thread

Make pattern pieces following diagrams. Cut two front/back pieces, two sleeves, two tails, four heads, four ears and two forehead pieces from fur fabric. 1cm seam allowance is included.

BODY

With right sides together, stitch front/back pieces together at inner leg seams. Trim and neaten seams. With right sides together, stitch front/back pieces together at centre back seam leaving a 4cm opening between dots for inserting tail. Stitch centre front seam below dot. Trim and neaten seams.

Cut 12cm strands of wool and stitch to curved end of one tail piece. With tail pieces right sides together and wool strands between fabric pieces, stitch around sides leaving straight edge open. Turn right side out, insert fibre filling. Insert tail into opening in centre back seam between dots, easing tail to fit. Stitch opening in seam closed, stitching twice to secure tail.

Turn in and stitch narrow hems along leg and neck edges or neaten with zigzag stitch. Cut two 20cm pieces of 10mm-wide elastic and stitch to sleeves as marked on diagram, stretching elastic as you sew.

With sleeve pieces folded right sides together, stitch underarm seams and around hand shaping. Trim, clip and neaten seams. Pin and stitch sleeves to body, right sides together. Trim and neaten seams.

Cut two 30cm pieces of 10mm-wide elastic. Stitch elastic around leg hems, stretching elastic as you sew. Attach 5mm-wide elastic around neck edge in same way.

Press under edges of front opening. Neaten raw edges with narrow hem or zigzag. Stitch hook and loop tape along front opening to form closure.

HOOD

With right sides together, stitch two head pieces together along curved centre seam, stitching from dot to lower edge. Stitch centre seam at chin. Repeat for remaining head pieces. Trim seams.

With right sides together, stitch forehead pieces to head sections matching dots. Trim and neaten seams.

With right sides together, stitch around two ear pieces leaving lower edge open. Turn right side out, pin and stitch 2.5cm-wide pleat in lower edge. Repeat for remaining ear pieces.

Neaten lower edge of ears with zigzag. Position ears on either side of forehead on one head section (this will be outer head). Pin and stitch ears in place.

Cut two eyes from white felt and glue in position on outer head. Glue plastic eyes on top of felt pieces. Attach plastic nose to outer head. Twist three or four pipe-cleaners together to form whiskers. Stitch to outer head just below nose.

With right sides together stitch outer head and lining pieces together around face opening. Clip and trim seam. Press seam allowance along lower edges of head and lining to wrong side. Turn lining to inside head and stitch lower edge of head and lining together.

Cut a 65cm strip of tape. Make looped fringe for mane by looping wool across tape and stitching, over wool, down centre of tape. Handstitch mane to head just behind ears.

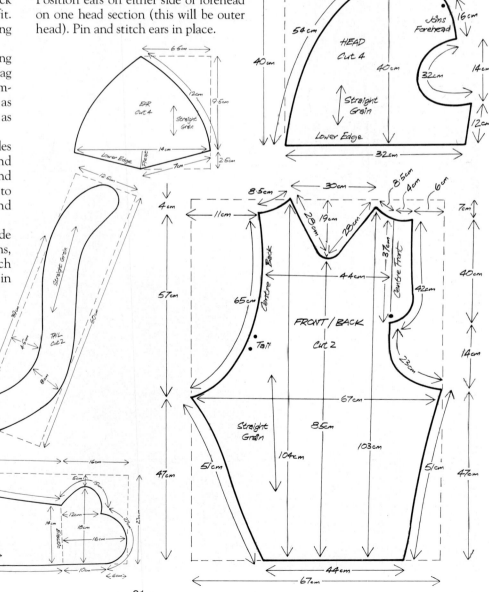

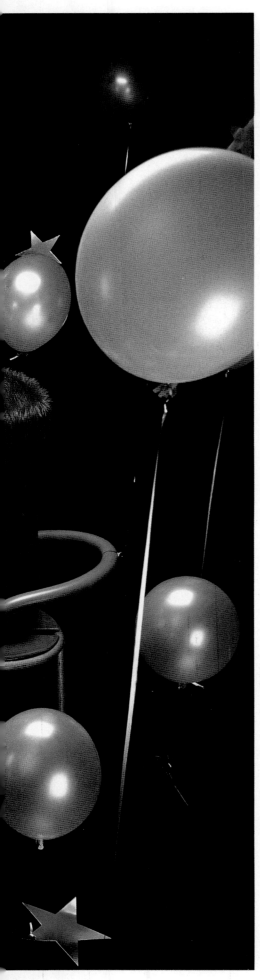

SPACED OUT

Every child is fascinated with the "final frontier" and with just a little imagination, silver paint and cardboard stars the universe can burst into your living room.

INVITATIONS

Star-shaped invitations may be the easiest or try a rocket shape and tie ribbons at the base. Always popular and very simple is a planet shape – brightly coloured. Alternatively, you may like to do an ordinary-shaped card and draw stars, comets and rockets on it, using glitter, of course.

DECORATIONS

Cut out stars and a large crescent moon, paint them silver and hang them from the ceiling (pieces of cotton and sticky tape or drawing pins will do the trick) or pin them to walls. Rockets made from cardboard tubes with cardboard wings and covered in aluminium foil look effective too. Cut dark blue cellophane into star and comet shapes and attach the shapes to windows. Fill some silver balloons with helium gas and tie with string attached to a weight on the floor.

All plastic plates, bowls, drink shakers, tray, jug: Decor Corporation

COSTUMES

Children would probably find it fun to dress up as their idea of what an alien would look like – a little green boy/girl or some weirdly wonderful creature. Other ideas include being an astronaut or perhaps the moon, sun or stars. Headdresses are good here. Cut out a cardboard sun or star (just half the shape), cut an arc in the bottom half to fit child's head, paint it gold and attach elastic to either side to go under child's chin.

The Golden Moon is a one-piece costume, with ties at the back. The blue eyes are net so the child can see well. The Alien is a one-piece lycra suit with a snaking spiral running down one side.

GAMES

● Try a variation on the old chocolate game. Children sit in a circle and take turns at rolling two dice until someone gets a double six. That person then has to run to the middle of the circle, get

LUNAR ROCKS

20g dark chocolate

1 cup Coco Pops

¼ cup chopped mixed nuts

1 cup pink and white marshmallows

¼ cup chopped red glace cherries

Melt chocolate in heatproof bowl over hot water, cool to room temperature.

Combine all ingredients in medium bowl. Mix well until ingredients are well combined.

Place tablespoonfuls of mixture onto a foil-lined tray. Chill until firm. Serve in a bed of icing sugar, if desired.

Makes 18.

dressed in a "space suit" (perhaps a ski suit with a bike helmet) and, using a knife and fork, try to open and eat a bar of chocolate ("space food"). The other children continue to throw the dice until another child throws a double six. He/she then runs to the middle and takes over the chocolate eating. The game ends when all the chocolate is eaten.

• Astronauts Race: Line children up and get them to "moonwalk" to the finish line. They need to walk in slow motion but they **must** keep moving at all times – the first past the line wins.

• Space Ball: Line children up and give each child a double page from a newspaper. They have until the count of five to decide how to scrunch up the paper and throw it the furthest. Mark each throw with a piece of paper – the furthest wins.

• Lunch in Space: Divide children into two teams. Spread several packets of Smarties or M and Ms out on a tablecloth or rug. Allot a colour to each child in the team, making sure two children (each from opposing teams) match. Appoint someone to call out colours (parent or other family member). When the colour is called the two children must collect their "lunch" on the teams' dinner plate as fast as they can using an ice-cream stick, as the caller counts to 10 or 20. The team with the most "lunch" is the winner.

GOODY BAGS

Try making some crescent or star-shaped chocolates (moulds are available), or scout around toy shops for rocket or shuttle toys or a selection of silver laser guns (water pistols). Modern cartoon-based toys and comics with a space theme also make ideal prizes. Present goodies wrapped in aluminium foil.

SPACE SHIPS

2 litres neapolitan ice-cream

12 flat-based coloured ice-cream cones

12 foil patty cake liners

¼ quantity Vienna cream, see glossary

food colouring, various colours

Soften ice-cream slightly. Using a spoon, fill each cone with a different coloured ice-cream. Place in freezer until firm.

Invert cones into flattened patty cake liners. Tint Vienna cream desired colours. Fill a piping bag with Vienna cream. Pipe planets or countries names onto cones. Return to the freezer.

Makes 12.

FLYING SAUCER SANDWICHES

12 shallots

12 pocket pita bread

12 lettuce leaves

12 slices ham

½ cup chopped celery

3 tomatoes, sliced

12 canned pineapple rings

48 cubes tasty cheese

toothpicks

10 pitted black olives, sliced

Using a sharp knife, shred one end of each shallot length, place in iced water to curl.

Fill bread with lettuce, ham and celery. Decorate top of bread with tomato, pineapple and shallot curls.

Secure cheese cubes with toothpicks to resemble landing legs. Sit bread onto landing legs with top of toothpick piercing bread. Secure olives on top of each toothpick.

Makes 12.

LEFT, TOP: Space Ball.
LEFT, CENTRE: Lunch in Space.
LEFT, BOTTOM: Astronauts Race.
ABOVE: Clockwise from front: Flying Saucer Sandwiches, Space Ships, UFO Cake, Lunar Rocks.

OUTER SPACE JUICE

6 canned pineapple rings

6 red glace cherries

2 litres lime soft drink

500ml pineapple juice

ice cubes

Place pineapple rings and cherries in drinking cups.

Pour in chilled lime soft drink, pineapple juice and ice cubes. Serve immediately.

Serves about 6.

UFO CAKE

2 x 340g packets chocolate
cake mix

1 quantity Vienna cream, see
glossary

black food colouring

assorted sweets

licorice

coloured pipe-cleaners

plastic toys

Make cakes according to directions on
packets. Spoon into a greased pudding
steamer (9 cup capacity). Bake in a
moderate oven for about 45 minutes or
until firm; cool on a wire rack. Place cake
onto prepared board. Tint Vienna cream
grey. Spread over cake, decorate with
assorted sweets, licorice, pipe-cleaners
and toys.

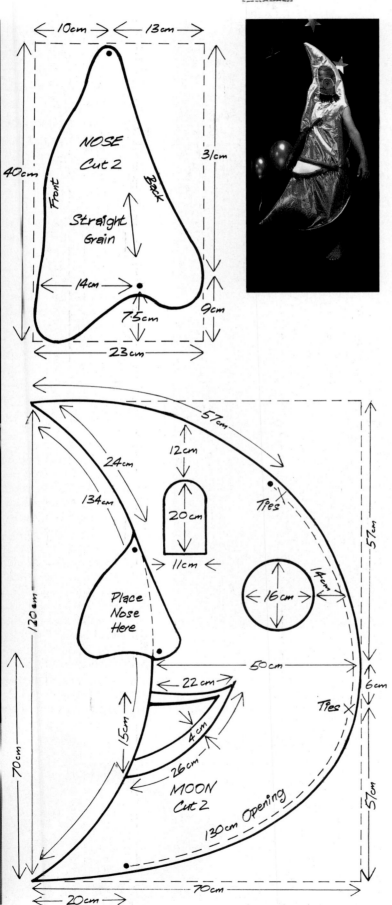

GOLDEN MOON

2.5m x 90cm-wide gold fabric

6mm-thick foam or 2.5m x 90cm-wide polyester wadding

scraps of tulle

scraps of yellow and black felt

2 black buttons

20cm x 115cm-wide pink fabric

1.4m cotton tape or ribbon

craft glue

thread

Make pattern following diagrams. Cut two moons and two noses from gold fabric. Cut two moons, two noses and one mouth from foam. 1cm seam allowance is included.

Tack foam to wrong side of gold moon pieces around edges. Cut out armholes and eyes and neaten edges.

With right sides together, stitch moon pieces together around front curved edge and back curve, leaving an opening between dots on back. Trim and neaten seams. Turn under and stitch a 1cm hem along edges of back opening.

Cut two rectangles of tulle slightly larger than eyes and glue or stitch to wrong side of eyes. Cut two yellow felt circles for eyes and stitch or glue to tulle. Stitch black buttons to centre of yellow felt. Cut two 12cm x 5cm pieces black felt. Cut into fringe leaving 1cm at top edge uncut. Glue uncut edge of felt below eyes for eyelashes.

With right sides together, stitch nose pieces between dots around front edge. Trim seam, turn right side out. Turn under and stitch hem along back edges. Pin and handstitch nose in position on front of moon matching dots.

Glue or stitch foam mouth piece in position under nose. Cut a 46cm x 8cm strip and a 54cm x 8cm strip pink fabric for lips. Cut foam pieces to correspond. With fabric and foam wrong sides together, roll strips into cylinders and glue to hold. Fold ends under and glue.

Glue longer strip around lower mouth edge and shorter strip to upper mouth edge for lips.

Cut tape or ribbon into four even lengths and stitch to edges of back opening for ties.

ALIEN COSTUME

1m x 150cm-wide brightly patterned lycra

30cm x 150cm-wide matching plain lycra

14cm hook and loop tape

polyester fibre filling

curling ribbon, in colours to match lycra

thread

Make pattern pieces following diagrams. Make hood pattern following diagram for Dragon Hood on page 61. Cut two front/backs, two sleeves and two hoods from patterned lycra. Cut three 10cm x 150cm strips from plain lycra. 1cm seam allowance is included. Use stretch or zigzag stitch.

With right sides together, stitch centre front and centre back seams, then stitch inside leg seam. Trim seam.

With right sides together, stitch underarm sleeve seams. Trim seams. Pin and stitch sleeves to body section, matching notches and leaving left front sleeve open 14cm from neck edge.

Stitch hook and loop tape to sleeve opening to form closure.

With right sides together, stitch hood pieces along centre back and chin seam. Trim seams, turn right side out.

Stitch two plain lycra strips together at ends to form one continuous strip. Fold strip in half lengthways, right sides together, and stitch across one end and down side. Turn right side out, insert fibre filling. Stitch end closed.

Pin and stitch strip to outfit, twisting it around body and stitching one end to body, one to leg. Stitch and fill remaining strip in same way. Stitch one end to hood, twist around hood and stitch the other end to one sleeve. Decorate hood with lengths of curling ribbon, as desired.

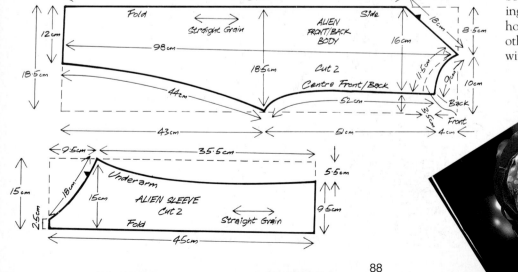

ALIEN FRONT/BACK BODY
Cut 2
Centre Front/Back

Fold · Straight Grain · Side · Back · Front

84cm · 14cm · 12cm · 18cm · 8.5cm · 98cm · 16cm · 18.5cm · 185cm · 11.5cm · 9cm · 10cm · 44cm · 52cm · 43cm · 51cm · 4cm

ALIEN SLEEVE
Cut 2
Underarm · Fold · Straight Grain

9.5cm · 35.5cm · 5.5cm · 15cm · 18cm · 15cm · 9.5cm · 25cm · 45cm

ANCHORS AWAY

This is the perfect theme for summer and great if you have a pool. If you do have a pool, you should tell children to bring their swimming costumes in the invitation. A nearby bay, lake or river will also provide a wonderful nautical backdrop.

Check with parents beforehand to find out whether their children can swim. Children are often boastful when asked about their swimming ability, especially if their friends are around. Of course, it is vital to have an adult (or two) present when children are swimming and at least one adult at the party who can do simple first-aid if an emergency arises.

Table and chairs: Cotswold Garden Furniture

Sandra
Come to a nautical party!
Date: 12th February
Time: 10am – Sunset
Place: Pier 1, St Mary's Wharf, Balmain,

GAMES

- Children may enjoy "fishing" with a rod and string with a magnet attached to the end of the string. Fill a bucket with small wrapped gifts with bottle tops attached to the wrapping. Children can each have a turn trying to "hook" one of the gifts with the magnet and bottle top.
- Marooned: Map out an island on the beach or in the garden using a towel or a rug. This is the "safe" place. Nominate one child to be the shark, the rest of the children are shipwrecked sailors. The shark chases the sailors and each one that is caught becomes a shark and helps catch the other sailors until the island is again deserted.
- Making Waves: Divide children into two teams. Line up each team at one end with a bucket of water and a small cup. Place an empty bucket about 15-20 metres away from the finishing line. Children have to take the water to the empty bucket, one by one. The team that empties their bucket first (using the cups!) is the winner.
- Treasure Hunt: Hide a booty of gold coins (chocolate ones of course) in the garden or at the beach. Draw a simple treasure map with an X marking where the treasure is buried. Give a map to each child and let the fun begin.

  If you'd prefer to keep it simple, hide the treasure, let the children search, and tell them when they are getting warmer (nearer the spot) or colder (moving away from the treasure).

INVITATIONS

Invitations can be made from coloured cardboard in the shape of a boat, a fish or a lighthouse. Alternatively, send out small plastic boats (bath toys) with the invitation on an attached card.

DECORATIONS

How about a blue and white theme? Use blue and white streamers around the house and perhaps cut shapes of fish out of cardboard and stick them on the walls, or hang blue and green streamers diagonally across the room and suspend fish, shells etc in the streamers to look like the sea.

Children may like to make their own simple boat hats by folding newspaper or blue paper.

If you have a beach or bay nearby make the most of it. Take some blue and white balloons along and tie them around to mark the party spot.

COSTUMES

Children could come dressed as sailors, swimmers or even fish. If you want to make it simpler, keep costumes to being just blue and white, striped or plain they'll look great.

GOODY BAGS

Any sort of bath toy is an ideal gift – a plastic boat or water animal such as a seal or turtle. Also good: bubble bath in lifebuoys or boats, Lifesaver sweets or a bandana filled with chocolate coins.

FISHERMAN'S CATCH

500g frozen french fries

24 fish fingers

12 cooked king prawns, peeled

6 parsley sprigs

6 lemon wedges

tartare sauce

Cook french fries in hot oil until golden, drain on absorbent paper. Grill, fry or bake fish fingers until tender.

Arrange french fries, fish fingers, prawns and parsley in serviette-lined baskets. Serve with lemon wedges, tartare sauce and bread rolls, if desired.

Serves 6.

SALMON AND CHEESE SAIL BOATS

4 sheets frozen shortcrust pastry

250g soft cream cheese

210g can pink salmon, drained and flaked

2 teaspoons lemon juice

freshly ground black pepper

8 cheese slices

toothpicks

Allow pastry to thaw to room temperature. Line greased pastry boat tins with thawed pastry. Place tins on oven trays. Bake in a moderate oven for 12 minutes or until golden and crisp. Allow to cool on wire racks.

Combine cream cheese, salmon, lemon juice and pepper. Spoon into pastry boats.

Cut cheese slices in half diagonally. Insert a toothpick into each and position in filled pastry boats to resemble a sail. Chill prior to serving.

Makes about 16.

DOUGHNUT LIFEBUOYS

1 quantity glace icing, see glossary

blue food colouring

12 plain doughnuts (without cinnamon and sugar coating)

Tint half glace icing blue. Decorate doughnuts with blue and white icing to look like lifebuoys. Allow to set.

Makes 12.

HOIST THE SAIL CAKE

340g packet buttercake mix

1 quantity Vienna cream, see glossary

brown food colouring

5 Flakes, roughly broken

bamboo skewers

piece of calico

plastic toys

Make cake following directions on packet. Spread mixture into a 20cm round cake pan. Bake in moderate oven for about 35 minutes or until firm; cool on a wire rack.

Cut cake in half, join halves together with Vienna cream. Trim base of cake so it will stand steadily. Place on prepared board. Tint Vienna cream brown. Spread cream evenly over sides of cake. Arrange Flake pieces on sides of cake. Decorate with a sail made from bamboo skewers and a torn piece of calico. Position toys on top of cake.

ABOVE, TOP: Front: Fisherman's Catch.
Front, left: Doughnut Lifebuoys,.
Centre, front: Hoist the Sail Cake.
Centre, back: Salmon and Cheese Sail Boats.
RIGHT: Hoist the Sail Cake.

BOAT AHOY

1.4m x 115cm-wide black fabric

60cm x 115cm-wide red fabric

80cm x 90cm-wide blue interlock

90cm x 115cm-wide stiff interfacing

60cm x 115cm-wide polyester wadding

40cm x 70cm-wide black ribbing

1 white felt square

grey felt scrap

20cm lightweight silver chain

2 x 25cm thin wooden battens

craft glue

Make pattern following diagrams. Cut four boat sides from black fabric. Cut two boat tops from red fabric. Cut two boat sides and one boat top from interfacing. Cut two boat sides from wadding. Cut two 100cm x 8cm straps from black fabric. 1cm seam allowance is included.

Apply interfacing to wrong side of one boat top piece. With wrong sides together, pin and stitch boat tops together around outer edges.

Stitch 40cm edges of ribbing right sides together. Fold ribbing with raw edges together to give a 20cm-wide tube. Pin and stitch ribbing around edge of circular cut-out on boat top, stretching ribbing to fit. Trim and neaten seam.

Apply interfacing to two boat side pieces. Pin and stitch wadding over interfacing. Stitch boat sides right sides together at ends. Stitch remaining boat sides together at ends. Tack boat side sections together around edges.

With right sides and raw edges together, pin and stitch boat top to top edge of sides. Make a 3cm-wide tuck around boat side, around top edge. Stitch tuck in place. Neaten lower edge of boat sides by zigzagging edges together.

Cut interlock fabric into two 83cm x 40cm pieces. Cut a fringe along one edge, leaving 10cm uncut at other edge. Stitch uncut edge around lower edge of boat sides.

Fold each strap in half lengthways, right sides together, stitch along sides and one end. Turn right side out, stitch ends closed. Pin on either side of cut-out on boat top, crossing straps. Fit on child, adjust strap length, stitch straps in place.

Cut circles from white felt for portholes and cut anchor from grey felt following actual size diagram. Glue portholes and anchor to side of boat. Stitch one end of chain to anchor and stitch other end to boat top.

Glue battens to inside of boat top across width of boat to give rigidity.

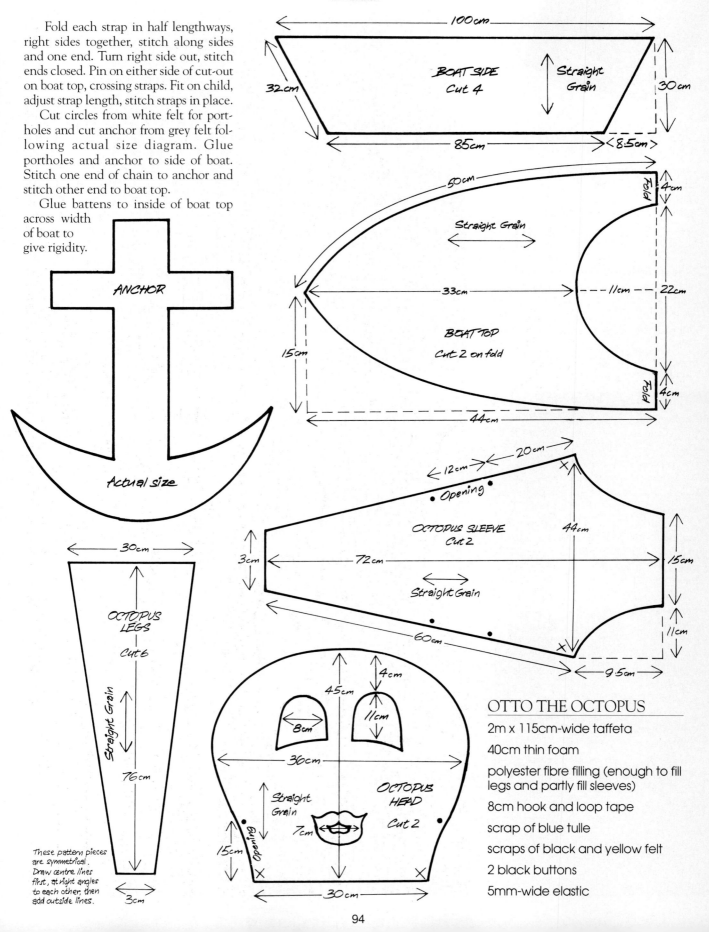

ANCHOR

Actual size

100cm

BOAT SIDE
Cut 4

Straight Grain

32cm

30cm

85cm

<8.5cm>

50cm

Fold

4cm

Straight Grain

33cm

11cm

22cm

BOAT TOP
Cut 2 on fold

15cm

Fold

4cm

44cm

12cm

20cm

Opening

OCTOPUS SLEEVE
Cut 2

44cm

3cm

72cm

15cm

Straight Grain

60cm

11cm

9.5cm

30cm

OCTOPUS
LEGS

Cut 6

Straight Grain

76cm

3cm

These pattern pieces are symmetrical. Draw centre lines first, at right angles to each other, then add outside lines.

45cm

4cm

8cm

11cm

36cm

Straight Grain

OCTOPUS
HEAD

Cut 2

Opening

7cm

15cm

30cm

OTTO THE OCTOPUS

2m x 115cm-wide taffeta

40cm thin foam

polyester fibre filling (enough to fill legs and partly fill sleeves)

8cm hook and loop tape

scrap of blue tulle

scraps of black and yellow felt

2 black buttons

5mm-wide elastic

Note. Costume may need to be adjusted to suit child's height. We made a fabric cape to wear underneath the octopus costume. Two rectangles of blue fabric were attached to a band and decorated with sheer fabric and strips of green and blue cellophane. Any blue or green clothing can be decorated in the same way to give the effect of the sea.

Make pattern following diagrams. Cut two heads, two sleeves and six legs from taffeta. Cut two heads from foam. 1cm seam allowance is included.

Tack foam to wrong sides of each head piece. Mark and cut out eyeholes following diagram. Cut two rectangles of tulle slightly larger than the eye area. Glue or stitch tulle to wrong side of head over eye cut-out. Zigzag around edges of eyes. With right sides together, stitch head pieces together leaving an opening along lower edge and at sides below dots. Trim and neaten seam. Turn right side out, turn under and stitch raw edges along lower edge and side openings.

Cut two circles from yellow felt and glue to tulle eye area. Stitch buttons in centre of felt. Cut 14cm x 10cm pieces black felt for eyelashes. Cut a fringe along one edge leaving 2cm uncut on other edge. Glue uncut edge around top edge of eye and glue tip of each eyelash above eye. Cut mouth from yellow felt, glue below eyes.

Fold each leg lengthways, raw edges and right sides together. Stitch leg seams to a point at bottom edge. Turn right side out, insert filling. Pin and stitch legs to lower edge of head, spacing them evenly.

With right sides together, stitch sleeve seam between Xs and lower edge, leaving openings for hands between dots. Turn under and neaten raw edges around sleeve tops between Xs. Turn right side out, lightly fill ends of sleeves, below openings, with fibre filling.

Fit the costume on the child and attach hook and loop tape to the upper sleeves and at top of armhole slits in side edge of head to correspond.

Cut two lengths of elastic and stitch one end of each piece to each bottom corner of head. (These loop under the child's arms to hold head in place).

Photography: Gerald Colley. Styling: Karen Byak

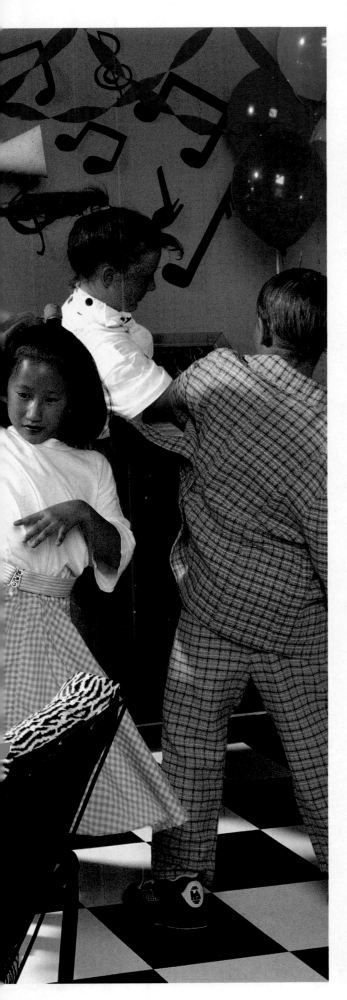

9 TO 12 YEARS

Children in the 9 to 12 age group are usually experienced party goers and givers, they know what they like and what they want, so listen to them. If you force a child to have a particular kind of party (i.e. the one YOU want) it will undoubtedly turn out to be a fizzer; kids at this age can be easily embarassed, especially if they have to do something they really don't want to.

✹ Get your children involved in the party preparations, deciding on decorations, invitations, food etc. If they express an interest, let them decorate the cake or even make it! It might be a little messy so make sure you start preparations early!

✹ Have some organised games up your sleeve; even children at the ripe old age of 12 enjoy games. Some may get a little nostalgic, too, about the games they played when they were young! It's not necessary to methodically go through each game listed. If the kids are enjoying themselves, let them go. But, don't let a game go on too long (10 minutes is a good rule of thumb). Here's where it gets a little tricky and you'll have to use your judgement on the day. Try not to halt the proceedings just because you think it's time for another game; that can be fatal.

✹ With this age group you have a little more scope with party times – these kids really enjoy an early evening party (Halloween is a perfect theme), it makes them feel more adult. And, the party can be longer (if parents can bear the thought!). Remember though, there CAN be too much of a good thing.

Jukebox: Music Hire Group; Amtico black and white floor tiles: Richard Cowell Interior Products; bowl, jug, platter: Guzzini, available from Novo Industries; helium balloons: Northside Balloons

TWIST AND SHOUT

Nine to 12-year-olds are very keen on the idea of disco and hard rock parties. They also love to indulge in nostalgia, asking their parents about the Beatles (which one did you like, Mum?), Marilyn Monroe, Elvis Presley and Buddy Holly. Ask them to bring a guitar, or any musical instrument, if they play it. Make sure the time for pick-up from the party is stated clearly.

INVITATIONS

Go to a second-hand shop and see if you can find some old 45 or 33 records. Use them to write the invitations on – either attach a piece of cardboard to the record with a paper clip or write on the label with a silver or gold pen. Otherwise, cut out black cardboard in the shape of a record and write the invitation on this. Hand deliver. Alternatively, draw a radio with musical notes coming out of it and write the invitation in the note bubbles.

DECORATIONS

If you have a romper room or large area where the children can dance, you might consider hiring a jukebox and some flashing lights for the night.

Posters of famous pop and movie stars, old and new, can be stuck up around the walls with Blu Tack.

Set up a bar or counter at one end of the room, away from the juke box. Here the children can help themselves to freshly-popped corn and drinks served in parfait glasses.

Foil balloons which say "Welcome to the 50s" can be obtained from specialist party shops; or just get a huge variety of balloons. Glossy paper bags with "the 50s" written on both sides are also available from party specialist shops, they could be used as loot bags.

The food table should be round, with a black tablecloth – in the shape of a record – and you can use old records as placemats; blow-out streamers can be strewn over the table

Play songs like *La Bamba, Jailhouse Rock and Rock Around the Clock* if it's a 50s party, anything by The Beatles, Herman's Hermits, or The Rolling Stones if it's a 60s party, and Abba, Bee Gees, Kiss, Sweet and Boney M songs for a 70s party.

COSTUMES

Girls should come in big skirts, bobby socks, scarves around their necks and hair tied back in a pony tail. Boys should wear rolled-up jeans and white socks, they can grease their hair and put duck tails at the back. Or they can come dressed as their favourite rock (or movie) star from the 50s and 60s.

GAMES

● Gossip (Chinese Whispers): The children sit in a circle and one child whispers a funny message to the next child who then repeats it to the next child until the message goes all the way around the circle. The last child repeats the message he/she heard out loud.
● Musical Bumps: Put on your favourite music. Children must run around until the music stops. As soon as the music stops they must sit down. The last one to sit down is out. On it goes until only one child is left. Or try Musical Statues in which the children dance around the room to music. When it stops they have to "freeze" and stand completely still. Anyone who moves is out.
● Charades: Divide the children into teams. Give each team a list of subjects – television shows, animals, books,

GOODY BAGS

Address books with rock stars on the cover, stickers of rock stars or film stars, miniature plastic guitars, red lipstick for the girls, hair oil for boys and lots and lots of bubblegum.

countries etc. Each team must act out their first title for the other team to guess. No-one is allowed to speak the words, it must all be done with gestures.

● Guess the Face: Pin the picture of a famous person on the back of each person. Everyone is given a clue and they have to guess who it is. The person who guesses first with the fewest clues wins.

● Jitterbug Competition: Children team up in pairs and dance until a pre-determined judge decides who are the best dancers.

● Matching Pictures: Find pictures of famous rock stars or movie stars, cut them in half, give each person half and get them to find the other half.

● Limbo: This is done to the song *Do the Limbo Rock*. Two people hold each end of a stick; the rest have to dance under it bent backwards. After everyone has had a turn, the stick is moved slowly lower and lower. Those who can't get under the stick are eliminated.

● Consequences: Everyone is given a pen and paper and they write a woman's name at the top. Each person then folds that down so what they have written can't be seen and passes it to the person on their right. Each person then writes down the name of a man. This continues until everyone has written:

- where they met
- what he said to her
- what she said to him
- what the consequence was
- any person's name
- what they said about the incident

The results are usually very amusing.

BELOW: Clockwise from back: Top of the Charts Cake, Limited Release Sandwiches, Hard-Boiled Rock Stars, Rock and Roll Guitars.

HARD-BOILED ROCK STARS

12 hard-boiled eggs

125g soft cream cheese

1 tablespoon dry French onion
soup mix

food colouring, various colours

alfalfa sprouts

shredded coconut

shallots

assorted vegetable pieces

sliced black olives

Peel eggs, trim bases of eggs so they stand
upright. Beat cream cheese and onion
soup mix together. Tint desired colours.
Place mixture into a greaseproof piping
bag. Pipe onto tops of eggs and pipe on
faces. Decorate with remaining ingredients to resemble groovy rock stars!

ROCK AND ROLL GUITARS

24 musk sticks

12 chocolate biscuits

12 licorice allsorts

1 licorice strand

100g dark chocolate

Trim musk sticks to even sizes. Lay biscuits out on a board or tray. Slice each
licorice allsort in half, thinly shred
licorice strand to even lengths.

Melt chocolate over pan of hot water,
spoon into a greased piping bag.

Using the chocolate as glue, fix 2
musk sticks, 1 licorice allsort and a shred
of licorice to each chocolate biscuit to
resemble a guitar. Chill in the
refrigerator until chocolate is firmly set.
Note. We trimmed our licorice allsorts
with scissors to resemble the centres of
real guitars.

LIMITED RELEASE SANDWICHES

24 slices bread

butter for spreading

selection of fillings: cheese and avocado; tomato, roast beef and lettuce; egg, shallots and lettuce; grated carrot, sultanas and cottage cheese; chicken, sprouts and tomato

Using a large round pastry cutter or the base of a large cup, cut bread into even rounds. Place half the rounds on a large foil-lined board. Cut a centre circle from each of the remaining rounds using a very small cutter or a bottletop as a guide.

Lightly butter all rounds. Fill with a selection of fillings. Place rounds with centre holes on top to resemble records.
Makes 12.

TOP OF THE CHARTS CAKE

2 x 340g packets chocolate cake mix

1 quantity Vienna cream, see glossary

black food colouring

single record (17.5cm size)

assorted sweets

cachous

Make cakes according to directions on packets. Spread mixture into 2 greased square 20cm cake pans. Bake in a moderate oven for about 35 minutes or until firm; cool on wire racks. Place cakes on prepared board. Join cakes with a little Vienna cream. Tint remaining cream grey. Spread over sides and top of cake. Smooth with a flat bladed knife.

Decorate cake with record, cachous and sweets to resemble a record player.

We topped our cake with a real record balanced on a licorice allsort. Place a little Vienna cream on top of licorice allsort to glue record in place. Chill in refrigerator.

RECORD HAT

1 discarded record

glue

crown of an old hat

rubber gloves

boiling water

Wearing rubber gloves, tip boiling water over the record and shape it to form wavy edges while it is soft. Repeat until you achieve the desired shape.

Glue the shaped record to the top of the hat crown.

LEFT: Top of the Charts Cake.

CIRCULAR SKIRT

2.8m x 90cm-wide fabric

5cm-wide elastic (length to fit child's waist)

felt and glitter pens

star- or heart-shaped sequins, for decoration

glue

Make pattern following diagram for Circular Skirt on page 75. Cut 2 fabric pieces. Stitch side seams and attach elastic as for Circular Skirt. Hem skirt edge.

Use felt pen to write names of singers or bands on the skirt. Decorate as desired with glitter pens. Glue on sequins.

BESIDE THE SEASIDE

You won't have much trouble convincing kids to enjoy this kind of party – the sun, sand, sea and surf will do it for you. It's a great theme for summer but remember, a winter beach party can also be loads of fun.

INVITATIONS

Cut out a large starfish, shell, palm tree or sandcastle from coloured cardboard and write details of place, time and date on the back. Tell guests to wear their brightest beach wear. If you can hand deliver the invitations, place a torn piece of paper with all the details inside a small bottle or fill a fabric bag with sand and party details and drop one off at each guest's house.

You are invited to a Beach Party
Date: 14th December
Time: 1pm – 6pm
Place: 1 Seaview Rd, Brighton
B.Y.O Bag o' Sand!

DECORATIONS

Set up a large pole (secured deep in the sand) festooned with balloons and streamers, so that guests can easily spot the party scene. Borrow some large sun umbrellas and have them set up before guests arrive; attach a few balloons to the tops of these. The kids will need some shelter from the sun when they settle down to eat.

Have lots of towels, sunblock and hats on hand and make sure you have an adequate supply of ice to keep drinks (and food) cool. Take a table on which to layout the food (keep it well sheltered from the sun), this will at least stop sand being kicked into the party food. Scatter some shells on the table or have food in those large (shop bought) shells. Take rugs or towels for the children to sit on and lay them under the umbrellas.

If you want to keep the food **really** simple, buy fish and chips (you could vary it with calamari, potato scallops etc.) from the nearest fish shop and lay it out for the kids on paper plates. Have paper towels or napkins for greasy fingers and cold drinks to wash it all down. Minimum of fuss and washing up!

COSTUMES

You could opt for a Hawaiian theme or a 50s beach party. Ask the children to wear Hawaiian shirts or shirts tied at the waist, cut-off, fringed shorts, board shorts or any beach gear. Oh, and make sure they bring their swimming costumes!

Buy some paper leis from a novelty shop or supermarket and hand them out to guests as they arrive, or before they attack the food table!

Have several pots of different coloured fluro zinc cream on hand to slather on faces when they arrive.

GAMES

You won't need to organise too many games as most of the fun is in swimming and playing in the sand and around the rockpools. Keep the children under close supervision.

● Make sure you have some beach balls around. Kids can play Piggy-in-the-Middle, French Cricket or any popular ball game. Try to get everyone to join in.

● Have a Limbo competition. Children dance under a pole (leaning backwards to fit under and not touching the ground) while the pole is gradually lowered. The last child to get under the pole without touching it or the ground is the winner.

● Organise a Sandcastle Building contest. The biggest, most elaborate, or the one left standing, wins.

● A Scavenger Hunt at the beach is always assured success. Ask the children to collect a list of things, for example 2 strange shells, 1 large shell, some seaweed etc. Each child should get a prize from their catch of the day.

● Invest in water pistols and let the children have a "shooting" competition.

GOODY BAGS

Bundle up some sea treasures in a plastic bucket or a sun hat/cap – pop in shell- or fish-shaped soap, jelly crocodiles, some pots of brightly coloured zinc cream, sun block, a blow-up beach ball and perhaps a plastic shark key ring or fridge magnet (something fishy if possible!).

SURFIE SAMS

250g butter

1 cup castor sugar

2 eggs, beaten

4 cups plain flour

1 quantity royal icing, see glossary

food colouring, various colours

licorice allsorts, sliced thinly

Cream butter and sugar together until light and fluffy. Add eggs, beat well. Stir in sifted flour. Mix well. Turn onto a floured board and knead lightly until mixture is smooth. Roll out thinly between two sheets of greaseproof paper. Cut out cookie man shapes using a gingerbread man cutter. Place onto greased oven trays and bake in a moderate oven for 12-15 minutes or until golden. Allow to cool on trays. Place on wire racks.

Tint icing desired colours, spoon into greaseproof piping bags, decorate biscuits with icing, fix licorice allsorts to biscuits using a little icing. Allow to harden before serving.

Makes about 16.

WIPE OUT CHICKEN AND CHIPS

18 chicken legs

2 tablespoons soy sauce

1 tablespoon vegetable oil

2 tablespoons pineapple juice

1 tablespoon tomato sauce

2 tablespoons honey

500g frozen french fries

oil for deep-frying

fresh parsley

Marinate chicken legs in combined soy sauce, oil, pineapple juice, tomato sauce and honey for 2 hours. Place legs into a greased baking dish, bake in a moderate oven for 40 minutes or until tender (brushing with marinade during cooking, if desired).

Deep-fry french fries in hot oil until golden and crisp, drain on absorbent paper. Serve hot with chicken legs, garnished with parsley.

Serves 6.

ABOVE: Clockwise from top: Mini Fruit Beach Balls, Wipe Out Chicken and Chips, Sandcastle Cake, Surfie Sams.

MINI FRUIT BEACH BALLS

1 watermelon

2 rockmelons

2 honeydew melons

Cut each melon in half. Using a melon baller, carefully remove balls from each. Place in a large bowl, chill. Spoon into beach buckets to serve.

    Serves 6.

SANDCASTLE CAKE

2 x 340g packets buttercake mix

1 quantity Vienna cream, see glossary

yellow food colouring

small flags

plastic toys

Make cakes according to directions on packets. Spoon mixture into a greased and floured Dolly Varden cake pan (10 cup capacity). Bake in a moderate oven for 40 minutes or until firm; cool on a wire rack. Place cake on prepared board, heavy side down. Using a small sharp knife, carefully cut windows in cake and small indents in top to resemble a castle.

    Tint Vienna cream yellow. Spread over sides and top of cake. Decorate with small flags and plastic toys.

BELOW: Sandcastle Cake.

IN THE WILD

This is a terrific idea for a party because it introduces children to the concept of preserving our trees and animals.

INVITATIONS

Invitations could be written on paper bags or recycled paper. Draw a green tree onto the paper and write:

> *"Wood you like to come
> to a party? I wood deerly like
> you to come dressed as
> your favourite tree or animal"*.

Alternatively, cut out the shape of an animal from cardboard and write party time, date and location on the body.

It might help to give children an idea of what to wear. Suggest a wattle tree, a Yeti, a Tasmanian Devil, a snow leopard and so on.

Come to my party dressed as a plant/animal

Date: 10 July   Time: 10am

Place: 6 Green Street Meadow-park.

DECORATIONS

Paw prints, sketched out in chalk, leading up to the front door, either along the garden path or outside on the footpath up to the gate. The paws could be tiger paws, Yeti paws or leopard paws. These can lead out to the clothes-line which could be draped with palm fronds or gum-tree branches to form a hut (green fabric is okay too). Parrot balloons can be hung on the hut (these are available from specialist party shops), or just make your own cardboard parrots.

The table, either inside or outside the hut should be covered with brown paper or recycled paper with drawings of trees or more paw prints.

Although initially a decoration, a pinata provides a fun game as well. A pinata in the shape of an animal could be made during the preceding week: Blow up a balloon and cover it with wet torn newspaper strips. Cover with wallpaper paste, then add another couple of layers, making sure the newspaper is wet beforehand. Let these three layers dry, then add another three layers, interspersed with more paste, and let those dry well too. The balloon could be shaped as a green turtle or frog – it can be painted or hung with green streamers made from crepe paper.

A small door is cut into the top of the pinata and the hollow insides filled with surprises. Fill the cavity with packets of seeds (for the garden), sunflower, sesame seeds and dried fruits tied in green cellophane for eating. In Mexico the pinatas are hung by a ribbon from the ceiling and the children "smash" them open with sticks.

GAMES

• Loggers vs. Greenies: The children line up in equal numbers on either side of a rope. A line is drawn in the middle and they pull and heave the rope until one side pulls the other across the line, or until one group falls to the ground.

• Pass the Snake: A version of Pass the Parcel. The snake is passed from one child to the next around a circle. Music is played in the background and when it is stopped, the child left holding the snake is counted out.

• Pencil and Paper Games: Give the children pen and paper and ask them to write down the different types of animals that live in trees while someone (parent or family member) counts to 30. Then get the children to write down all the things that are made from trees (matchsticks, tables, floors etc). Finally, ask the children to write down the names of as many different types of trees as possible. The one with the most names in each section wins – that's three prizes to give out.

• Traditional games like Leapfrog (Leapturtle), Piggyback Races, What's the Time, Mr Wolf?, and Hunt the Turtle also work well.

GOODY BAGS

In a small hessian bag or a brown paper bag tied with string, place some green lollies, green scrunchies, a cupcake or doughnut with green icing, plastic animal keyrings or animal-shaped soap.

Tumbler, bowl: Guzzini, available from Novo Industries

WHALE OF A FRUIT SALAD

1 small round watermelon

assorted fruits: berries, grapes, bananas and peaches, peeled, cubed

Place watermelon on a flat surface. Draw a tail and round whale head design on skin with a pen. Using a sharp knife cut around design. Remove skin in pieces. Scoop out flesh leaving a 3cm thick wall. Reserve watermelon flesh. Make into balls using melon baller.

Cut out eyes and nose. Fill whale with prepared fruit and watermelon.

BELOW: Clockwise from front: Forest Green Sandwiches, Whale of a Fruit Salad, Global Wildlife Cake, Ozone Layer Sunday.

FOREST GREEN SANDWICHES

6 slices wholegrain bread

butter for spreading

alfalfa sprouts

2 avocados, peeled, sliced

snowpea sprouts

1 green capsicum, sliced

1 bunch asparagus, blanched

Lightly butter all bread. Fill sandwich with alfalfa, avocado, snowpea sprouts, capsicum and asparagus.

Cut in half diagonally and serve. Makes 6 halves.

OZONE LAYER SUNDAE

85g packet lime jelly crystals

2 cups marshmallows

12 scoops chocolate ice-cream

3 bananas, peeled, sliced

6 Flakes

Make jelly according to directions on packet. Allow to set. Chop jelly roughly, place in a serving dish with marshmallows, ice-cream and bananas. Cut Flakes in half, decorate with Flakes.
Note. This can be made into individual sundaes, if desired.
Makes 6.

GLOBAL WILDLIFE CAKE

2 x 340g packets buttercake mix

1 quantity Vienna cream, see glossary

blue and green food colourings

plastic trees, animals and birds

Make cakes according to directions on packets. Spread into 2 greased litre pudding basins. Bake in a moderate oven for about 35 minutes or until firm; cool on wire racks. Place on prepared board or plate. Join cakes with a little Vienna cream.

Tint ½ cup Vienna cream blue and the remaining cream green. Spread cream onto cake to resemble a world globe. Decorate with plastic trees, animals and birds.

PETAL HEADS

These foam flower decorations are simple to make. We used a piece of foam 100cm-square and 3cm-thick and cut the flower shapes with a sharp craft knife (you can use scissors). We cut a hole in the centre of the flower to fit around the child's face. The flower petals were painted with spray paint; paint could also be applied with a sponge.

LEFT: Global Wildlife Cake.

"Double, double toil and trouble
Fire, burn; and, cauldron, bubble.
Fillet of a fenny snake,
In the cauldron boil and bake;
Eye of newt, and toe of frog,
Wool of bat, and tongue of dog,
Adder's fork, and blind-worm's sting.
Lizard's leg, and howlet's wing,—
For a charm of powerful trouble,
Like a hell-broth, boil and bubble.
Double, double toil and trouble;
Fire, burn; and cauldron, bubble."
— Shakespeare

TRICK OR TREAT

Halloween has become very popular in Australia over the
past few years. Children find it a rich source of ideas for
dressing up, playing pranks and having all sorts of ghoulish
fun. The "spooky" element obviously appeals.

Date: 31st Oct
Time 5p.m – 9pm
Place: 10 Salem Cres

Peter Mulrooney

INVITATIONS

Fold a piece of orange cardboard in half and trace out the shape of a pumpkin. Write the name of the person invited on the front, details of the party: date, time (start and finish) and what to wear. Ask them to bring along some small "treats". Or, buy little golden nugget pumpkins and tie their stalks with a black ribbon. Write party details in black thick felt-tip pen onto the skin of the pumpkins. Don't forget to mention the "treats". Deliver the invitations personally.

DECORATIONS

One or two large pumpkins carved in the shape of Jack O'Lanterns. An adult should do this as the pumpkins can be hard to cut. Use a triangle shape for the eyes and nose, and a wide grinning mouth. A candle can be set inside so that the pumpkin glows. Put one at the front door, and one in the centre of the birthday table.

Tie a sheet around a large balloon, using a black ribbon, draw in black eyes and hang the "ghost" in one of your front windows.

Fill the centre of the table with little golden nugget pumpkins – and any other interestingly shaped pumpkins which can be found. Use black napkins and straws, orange cups and try to keep everything black, orange or white. Light the table with candles and let the children sit around and tell ghost stories.

Make witches hats out of small semi-circles of black paper and stick them onto the small pumpkins.

COSTUMES

Suggest the children come dressed as a black cat (black leotard and whiskers painted on their face, a witch (with a broomstick and hat), a ghost (use a white sheet, cut out holes for eyes, draw around holes), a devil (red leotard and cape, painted face and a three-pronged cardboard fork). Colour their hair green or orange or black (if they are blonde) with spray-on hair colour, to make them look like a Halloween monster.

GAMES

● Trick or Treat: The idea behind this game is "either you give me a treat or I'll play a trick on you." Two children, dressed up as demons, dragons, witches or ghosts, and carrying sacks, go around to the others and ask for one of their "treats". If the children say "no" (or have forgotten to bring their treats with them), then the demons play a trick on that child.

● Bobbing Apples: Any number can play this game, but hands must be behind backs. Tie string to the stalks of apples and hang them from a stick suspended horizontally, about 3 metres off the ground. The apples swing back and forth as each person tries to take a bite. Alternatively, put the apples into a tub of water. With hands again held behind their backs, the children try to catch one in their teeth.

Try also passing an apple from one person to another. Children must hold the apple under their chin and pass it to the next child who must take it under their chin too.

● Poison: Any number can play this game. Play Alice Cooper's song *Poison* in the background. Put a large preserving pan or witches pot on the floor (fill it with plastic snakes, frogs, spiders). Ask five or more people to join hands, forming a circle around the pot. One person is chosen to be leader. He or she tries pushing or pulling the other players so that one of them knocks his foot against the pot. As soon as this happens, that player is called "poison" and all the other players run away from him. The player who is "poison" chases them until he catches someone and that person then becomes leader. Everyone joins hands in a circle again and the new leader tries to get someone else to touch the pot and become "poison".

● Hunt the Frog: A variation of Hunt the Thimble. One child hides a plastic

frog in a room or in the garden so that it is camouflaged but not impossible to find. The rest of the children come to find the frog. The first child to find the frog wins a prize.

● Tell ghost stories.

GOODY BAGS

Choose from a selection of plastic spiders, sparklers, books of ghost stories and small bottles of bubble bath relabelled Blood Bath or Witches' Beauty Treatment. Wrap up the goodies in orange cellophane tied with a thick black ribbon.

WITCHES BREW

½ cup cocoa

½ cup castor sugar

2 teaspoons cinnamon

250ml hot water

200ml orange juice

2 litres milk

Combine cocoa, sugar, cinnamon and water in a saucepan. Stir over low heat until sugar dissolves. Add orange juice and milk. Do not allow to boil. Serve warm from the saucepan or from a black cast iron pot.

Serves 6.

TRICK OR TREAT JAM TARTS

12 frozen shortcrust pastry cases

Choc Bits

1 cup strawberry jam

300ml carton thickened cream

licorice allsorts

Place frozen pastry cases in individual foil cases on oven trays. Fill 6 cases with Choc Bits. Spoon a tablespoon of jam into each case. (Those cases with Choc Bits are the treats!). Bake in a moderate oven for 15 minutes or until golden. Remove and allow to cool in foil cases on a wire rack.

Whip cream, spoon into a piping bag. Decorate each tart with cream and sliced licorice allsorts.

Makes 12.

JAFFA LANTERNS

12 oranges

2 litres chocolate ice-cream

3 Flakes

Cut tops off oranges. Remove orange pulp from each, leaving a thick shell. Remove pulp from orange top, cut a hole in each top; discard pulp. Using a sharp knife cut faces into sides of each orange shell. Spoon in ice-cream. Replace top of orange. Cut each Flake into quarters. Insert a piece of Flake into each hole in the orange tops. Wrap individually in foil. Freeze for at least 3 hours.

Makes 12.

SPOOKY SPUDS

6 medium washed potatoes

6 sheets filo pastry

¼ cup melted butter

tomato sauce

sour cream

Peel potatoes, wash and drain well. Place in a lightly greased baking dish. Bake in a moderate oven for 50 minutes, turning occasionally. Remove, allow to cool slightly. Slice a small piece off the base of each potato so each stands up securely.

Brush each filo pastry sheet with melted butter, fold in half and place over potato. Brush with butter again. Place on greased oven trays. Make eyes in pastry using the point of a sharp knife. Bake in a moderately hot oven for about 15 minutes or until golden. Serve with tomato sauce and sour cream, if desired.

Makes 6.

HALLOWEEN CAKE

2 x 340g packets chocolate cake mix

1 quantity Vienna cream, see glossary

orange food colouring

licorice pieces

Make cakes according to directions on packets. Spread mixture into 2 greased 20cm round cake pans. Bake in a moderate oven for about 35 minutes or until firm; cool on a wire rack. Place cakes on prepared board or plate.

Join cakes with a little Vienna cream. Tint remaining cream bright orange. Spread over sides and top of cake. Decorate with licorice to resemble a traditional Halloween Jack O'Lantern.

LEFT: Halloween Cake.
ABOVE: Clockwise from back: Witches Brew, Jaffa Lanterns, Halloween Cake, Trick or Treat Jam Tarts, Spooky Spuds.
Guzzini platter: Novo Industries

OLD HAG'S COSTUME

2m black tulle

2m x 2cm-wide grosgrain ribbon

silver felt pen

craft glue

rubber or plastic spiders, bats, skeletons, mice, snakes

novelty spider webs (available at novelty and party supply stores)

old black felt hat

black tights

black skivvy

wicker basket *or* pot

thread

CAPE

Make cape pattern following diagram on page 80. Cut six cape pieces from tulle. Stitch pairs of cape pieces together at centre back seam.

Place cape pieces on top of each other to give three layers, stitch together at neck edge. Bind raw neck edge with ribbon, centring ribbon to form ties at centre front edges (to tie around child's neck). If desired, knot ends of ribbon.

Cut ragged edges around bottom of cape. Decorate cape with silver felt pen. Glue spider webs, plastic spiders etc onto cape.

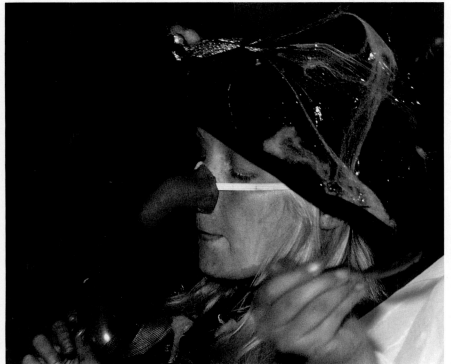

HAT

Hold an old felt hat over steam and shape it as desired. (Be careful to wear protective clothing to avoid burns). The point on our hat was made by steaming the hat then pushing a broom handle into the crown. The steaming and moulding process was repeated several times until the desired shape was achieved. Decorate with spider webs and other plastic creatures.

TIGHTS AND SKIVVY

Using the silver felt pen, draw patterns and shapes on the tights and skivvy. Glue on spider webs and other novelties.

BASKET/CAULDRON

Drape basket or pot with spider webs. Tie or glue on plastic spiders, flies, rubber bats and snakes.

THE PYJAMA GAME

Sleepovers are very popular with the 9 to 12-year-olds, though it is best to keep it to either all girls or all boys. The children will make sure of this anyway.

In summer, put up a tent in the backyard and let the children sleep outside under the real stars.

It can be fun to combine a sleepover with a magic theme: ask the children to bring a top hat, magician's cloak and wand. You supply the white rabbit (a toy will suffice) and a few packs of cards.

INVITATIONS

Buy some sheets of strong cardboard and cut out star shapes. Write the details for the birthday party onto these, giving the date, time and what to bring. For a sleepover, it would be wise to suggest bringing a sleeping bag, nightie, pyjamas and toothbrush. Organising the time of pick-up is most important.

The stars can be made of white cardboard and sprinkled with silver glitter – just use a little glue for this. Or you can stick small silver stars (available from newsagents) onto the bigger star.

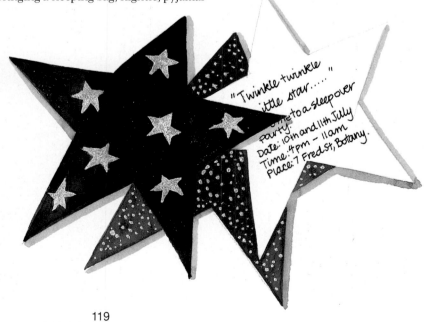

DECORATIONS

Make more cardboard stars, sprinkle with glitter, and suspend them with wool or string from the roof of the bedroom.

Buy packets of small luminous stars with adhesive backs (available from gift shops) and stick them onto the ceiling; there are "Starlight Zones", "Solar Systems" and "Glow in the Dark" moons available (games shops stock these).

Sprinkle the food table randomly with small multi-coloured stars (available in packets from newsagents). Stuff paper napkins with stars; they will fall out when your guests open them.

COSTUMES

Tell the kids to wear any kind of whacky pyjamas – their parents' or their own – nightshirts, long pyjamas, baby doll pyjamas or nightdresses. Supply them with Wee Willy Winkie style caps.

Sleeping bags and rug: Tramping 'n' Camping

GAMES

The child that arrives first is nominated "fairy godmother" or "fairy godfather" for the night – that person is given a wand and is put in charge of putting a "spell" on the children to send them off to sleep when it is time, using various spells, bedtime stories or fierce orders.

● If the children are sleeping in beds, they can "short-sheet" them.

● Plastic spiders or frogs and rattly bamboo snakes can be placed in the bottoms of sleeping bags.

● Choose a person to be "it". Begin a normal conversation, "it" is not allowed to say yes, no or grunt for an answer. If they do, they must choose another person to be "it". The person who lasts the longest as "it" wins a small prize.

● Fortune Telling: One of the girls can dress up as a gypsy (a bright scarf to pull her hair back, large circular hanging earrings, a wide skirt and colourful top). She can "read" tea leaves or "read" your palm, making it up as she goes. Have songs like *That Old Black Magic* or *Black Magic Woman* or *Witch Queen of New Orleans* playing in the background.

● Modelling balloons: You can buy these long thin balloons from party shops. Give two or three to each child and ask them to "model" different shapes.

● Flour-dipping: Fill a large bowl with plain white flour and put a silver coin or some other small gift into it. The idea is to find the treasure by dipping your face into the flour and finding it with your tongue. No hands allowed! Best done outside to avoid mess.

● If it's an all girls party, be sure to provide a range of lurid nail polishes: – glitter, fluro, black, blood red – plus nail files and other manicure accessories. Old lipsticks, eyeshadow, rouge or powder compacts can also provide hours of fun. Remember to have a generous stock of nail polish and eye-makeup remover, skin cleanser, cotton balls and hand cream in the cupboard. Have some fashion and pop magazines on hand for the girls to spend hours with.

GOODY BAGS

In a large bedsock place the matching bedsock, a gingerbread person and a candle (to light you to bed).

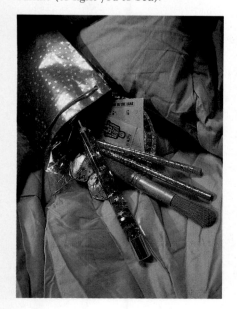

HEAVENLY CHEESE BITES

60g butter

¼ cup grated tasty cheese

2 tablespoons milk

1 cup plain flour

salt and pepper

Mix butter and cheese together. Stir in milk, flour and salt and pepper to taste. Mix to a soft dough, turn onto a floured surface and knead lightly. Roll out thinly between two sheets of greaseproof paper. Cut into star and moon shapes. Brush with milk. Place onto greased oven trays, bake in a moderate oven for 15 minutes. Remove from oven, allow to cool on trays.

We served our Heavenly Cheese Bites with a dip made up from a 16g dry dip mix blended with a 300g carton of sour cream.

Makes about 24.

BYE-BYE BREAD

18 slices white bread

butter for spreading

½ cup hundreds and thousands

12 marshmallows

100g dark chocolate

Remove crusts from bread, discard crusts. Lightly butter bread. Cut 6 slices of bread in half, sprinkle hundreds and thousands on buttered side. Position sprinkled bread on buttered side of larger bread slices. Place a marshmallow at centre top of each "bed" to form head.

Melt chocolate over pan of hot water, spoon into a greased piping bag. Decorate marshmallows with chocolate faces. Chill until set.

Makes 12.

ABOVE: Clockwise from back: Starry Night Cake, Heavenly Cheese Bites, Sweet Crescent Moons, Bye-Bye Bread.

SWEET CRESCENT MOONS

3 sheets frozen puff pastry

125g soft cream cheese

1 egg yolk

pink cake sprinkles

Allow pastry to thaw to room temperature. Cut into rounds using a fluted 6cm round cutter. Place a small teaspoon of cream cheese in the centre of each round. Brush edges with beaten egg yolk, press edges together firmly. Place onto lightly greased oven trays. Brush tops with egg yolk and bake in a hot oven for 8 minutes or until golden. Cool on wire racks. Place remaining cream cheese in a greaseproof piping bag. Pipe a small amount on top of cooled pastry moons. Dip cream cheese in cake sprinkles. Chill until firm.

Makes about 18.

STARRY NIGHT CAKE

340g packet buttercake mix

1 quantity Vienna cream, see glossary

yellow food colouring

cachous

Make cake according to directions on packet. Spread mixture into a greased star-shaped cake pan. Bake in a moderate oven for about 25 minutes or until firm; cool on a wire rack. Place cake on prepared board. Tint Vienna cream yellow. Spread over top and sides of cake. Decorate with cachous.

Note. Star-shaped cake pans are available from large department stores and kitchen specialty shops.

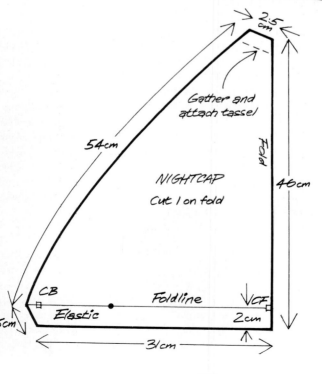

LEFT: Starry Night Cake.

Diagram labels:
2.5 cm
54cm
Gather and attach tassel
NIGHTCAP
Cut 1 on fold
Fold
46cm
CB
Foldline
CF
Elastic
2.5cm
2cm
31cm

NIGHTCAP

50cm x 115cm-wide fabric

purchased tassel or wool

15cm x 7mm-wide elastic

thread

Make pattern following diagram. Cut one nightcap piece using pattern.

With right sides together, stitch, trim and neaten back seam.

Turn up and press fabric to wrong side along bottom foldline. Machine stitch close to both folded edges.

Zigzag elastic to fabric between dots on inside of cap along back foldline, stretching elastic to fit.

Stitch a gathering thread along broken line. Pull up and secure gathers.

Turn cap right side out. Stitch tassel to top of cap or make and attach a woollen tassel.

GLOSSARY

Some terms, names, alternatives and basic recipes are included here to help everyone understand and use the recipes in this book successfully.

Almonds, Flaked: blanched almonds sliced horizontally.

Bacon Rashers: bacon slices.

Baking Powder: a raising agent consisting of an alkali and an acid. It is mostly made from cream of tartar and bicarbonate of soda in the proportions of 1 level teaspoon cream of tartar to ½ level teaspoon bicarbonate of soda. This is equivalent to 2 teaspoons baking powder. Sift ingredients several times before using.

Bamboo Skewers: can be used instead of metal skewers if soaked in water overnight or for several hours to prevent burning during cooking. They are available in several different lengths.

BASIC BUTTER CAKE

125g butter
1 teaspoon vanilla essence
½ cup castor sugar
2 eggs
1½ cups self-raising flour
½ cup milk

Cream butter, essence and sugar in small bowl with electric mixer until light and fluffy; beat in 1 egg at a time, until combined. Stir in sifted flour and milk in 2 batches. Spread mixture into prepared pans. Bake in moderate oven for 25 minutes or until firm; cool on wire rack.
Note: if using mixture as 1 whole cake, bake in moderate oven for 50 minutes or until firm.

BASIC SPONGE

This recipe does not contain any liquid.

3 eggs
½ cup castor sugar
¼ cup cornflour
¼ cup plain flour
¼ cup self-raising flour

Eggs should be at room temperature. Beat whole eggs in small bowl with electric mixer on moderately high speed until thick and creamy; about 7 minutes. Add sugar 1 tablespoon at a time, beating after each addition until sugar is dissolved. Sift dry ingredients together 3 times. When sugar is dissolved transfer mixture to large bowl. Sift flours over egg mixture, fold in lightly. Spread mixture into prepared pans. Bake in moderate oven for 20-25 minutes or until springy to the touch; cool on wire rack.

Note: if using mixture as 1 whole cake, bake in a moderate oven for 45-50 minutes or until firm to the touch.

Beef Burgers: we used I & J's frozen 300g Big Beefers (6 in a packet) you may prefer to make your own beef rissoles.

Bicarbonate of Soda: baking soda.

BISCUITS:

Plain: we used Shredded Wheatmeal, you may use any round plain biscuit of your choice.

Chocolate: we used Weston's Concerto soft cream centre biscuit. Any chocolate-coated round biscuit can be used.

BREADCRUMBS:

Stale: use 1 or 2 day old white or wholemeal bread made into crumbs by grating, blending or processing.

Packaged: use commmercially packaged breadcrumbs or cornflake crumbs.

Butter: use salted or unsalted (sweet) butter; 125g is equal to 1 stick butter.

Cachous: small round cake-decorating sweets, available in silver, gold or colours.

Cake Boards: we have indicated in recipes when to position cakes on boards as most people will want to present the cakes on a board, platter or plate, etc.

Check the cake pans or cut a paper pattern to help you get the right size. Allow extra space for frostings and decorations.

The board should be covered with some sort of greaseproof paper. Special paper is available from cake decorators suppliers or you can use certain gift paper such as a thin patterned aluminium foil. Kitchen-type aluminium foil is also ideal.

To cover a round board, snip paper shape at intervals, as shown. Fold over and tape securely to board.

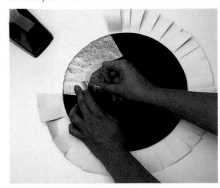

To cover square board, cut paper to size, neaten corners and tape securely to board, as shown.

Cake Crumbs, How to Avoid: to keep the cake as neat as possible, bake the cake a day before you decorate it. After cooling, keep it in an airtight container in the refrigerator overnight.

Decorate the cake while it is cold or, if you think you are going to take more than about 30 minutes, freeze the cake, uncovered, for 30 minutes, then decorate. This will not eliminate the crumb problem but will certainly help.

Cake Pans, How to Grease: we used a pastry brush to grease cake pans lightly but evenly with a little melted butter. Some people prefer to line the base of cake pans with greaseproof or baking paper; it's a matter of choice. We dusted greased aluminium pudding steamers and Dolly Varden pans with flour, then shook out the excess.

CHEESE:

Cream Cheese: also known as Philly.

Soft Cream Cheese: commercially softened spreadable Philly bought in tubs.

Tasty: we used a hard cheddar cheese.

Slices: commercially bought processed cheese slices available in tasty or cheddar.

Cherry Tomatoes: small bite-sized round red tomatoes.

Chicken: numbers indicate the weight. For example: No. 13 chicken weighs 1.3kg. This applies to all poultry.

Choc Bits: buds of dark chocolate.

CHOCOLATE:

Dark: we used best eating quality, dark block chocolate.

Grated: use a kitchen grater (or vegetable peeler to make curls).

Chocolate, How to Melt: Use a double saucepan or a heatproof bowl over a saucepan of water. Place chocolate in top of the saucepan or the bowl and set it aside. Put water in bottom half of the saucepan, but not enough to touch the base of the top saucepan or bowl. Bring water to boil, remove from heat, then immediately place the chocolate in its saucepan or bowl over the hot water. Leave to stand, stirring occasionally, until the chocolate is melted. DO NOT melt chocolate by itself over direct heat.
DO NOT allow water to come into contact with chocolate when it is heating. Just a drop of water is the danger; a large amount of liquid usually blends in smoothly.
DO NOT cover the bowl containing the chocolate or condensation will form; water will drop into the chocolate and ruin it.
DO NOT overheat chocolate. If this happens and the chocolate turns from a glossy, liquid mass to a dull coarse-textured mess, you will have to discard the chocolate and start again. Leftover chocolate which has been melted properly can be re-melted over and over again.
Chocolate Topping: a chocolate syrup used in milk drinks or on ice-cream.
Cinnamon: fragrant bark used as a spice in ground form or sticks (quills).
Cocktail Frankfurts: baby frankfurts.
Cocoa: cocoa powder.
COCONUT: use desiccated coconut unless otherwise stated.
  Flaked: coconut flesh that has been flaked and dried.
  Shredded: thin strips of coconut.
Coconut, How to Colour: place coconut in plastic bag, add a drop or two of liquid colouring, knead colouring through coconut by pressing and pushing the bag. Keep leftover coconut in airtight container in refrigerator.

Coco Pops: chocolate-flavoured rice crispies.
Colourings: we used concentrated liquid vegetable food colourings and edible

powder colourings. The powder form gives best results for strong, bold colours.
Copha: a solid white shortening based on coconut oil. Kremelta and Palmin can be substituted.
CREAM: is simply a light pouring cream, also known as half'n'half.
  Sour Cream: a thick commercially cultured soured cream.
  Thickened (whipping) Cream: is specified when necessary in recipes.
  Whipped: thickened cream beaten until light and fluffy.
Crushed Nuts: crushed peanuts.

Decorations: if placing trimmings, such as lace, braid and ribbon, etc on a cake with Vienna cream, position them at the last minute as the butter from the cream will discolour any fabric.
Dried Mixed Herbs: commercially bought dried combination of thyme leaves, rosemary leaves, marjoram leaves, basil leaves, oregano leaves and sage leaves.
Drumstick: section cut from first joint of the chicken leg.

Filo Pastry: thin sheets of pastry available refrigerated or frozen. It dries out rapidly so cover pastry with plastic wrap or damp tea-towel to prevent drying out while using.
Fish Fingers: frozen finger-sized rectangles of fish crumbed ready for frying, grilling or baking.
Flake: light flaky 30g milk chocolate bar.
FLOUR
  White Plain: all purpose flour.
  White Self-Raising: substitute plain (all-purpose flour and baking powder in the proportion of 3/4 metric cup plain flour to 2 level metric teaspoons baking powder; sift together several times before using. If using an 8oz measuring cup, use 1 cup plain flour to 2 level metric teaspoons baking powder.
  Cornflour: cornstarch.

Golden Syrup: a golden-coloured syrup made from sugar cane. Maple, pancake syrup or honey can be substituted.
Glace Cherries: cherries cooked in sugar syrup then coloured red.

GLACE ICING
¾ cup icing sugar
½ teaspoon butter
2 teaspoons water, approximately
Sift icing sugar into a small heatproof bowl, stir in butter and enough water to give a stiff paste. Place bowl over a saucepan of simmering water, stir constantly until icing is just warm and runny; do not overheat or icing will crystalise. Tint desired colour.

Grill, Griller: broil, broiler.
Ground Ginger: powdered dried ginger root.

Honey Smacks: puffed wheat breakfast cereal toasted in honey.
Hundreds and Thousands: nonpareils.

ICE CREAM CONES: available in a range of colours.
  Ice-Cream Cones, Sugar: wafer type cones available in supermarkets.

Jaffas: red candy-coated milk chocolate balls.
Jam: a preserve of sugar and fruit.
Jelly Beans: small bean-shaped sweets available in a range of colours.
Jelly Crystals: fruit-flavoured gelatine crystals available from supermarkets.
Jubes: soft sweets available in various shapes. Can be sugar-coated.

Levelling Cakes: most cake mixtures rise unevenly or to a peak, particularly those cooked in loaf, bar and round pans. In most cases, the top needs to be cut off so the icing will sit flat or the cake will join smoothly to other cakes.
LICORICE: An aniseed confection which comes in straps, tubes and twisted ropes.
  Allsorts: layered sweets consisting of licorice and fondant.
  Straps: about 40cm flat lengths.

Marshmallows: we used packaged round marshmallows coloured pink or white.
Milk: we used full cream milk.
Musk Stick: musk-flavoured fondant.

Neapolitan Ice-Cream: strawberry, chocolate and vanilla ice-cream sold in one container.

Patty Cake Liners: individual paper patty cases (also available in foil) used for small cakes and sweets; available in supermarkets.
Peanut Butter: peanuts ground to a paste, available in crunchy and smooth.
Piping Bag: if you don't have a readymade piping bag, it's simple to make your own from greaseproof or baking paper. You don't need tubes, cut a hole at the piping end. Cut a triangle shape from paper and twist into a cone shape as shown.

Fill cone with Vienna cream.

Fold end of cone over to keep cream contained in piping bag.

Hold bag for piping as shown; squeeze gently but firmly.

Pocket Bread: small circles of Lebanese pita bread.
Potato Chips: potato crisps.
Puff Pastry: available from supermarkets in blocks and in ready-rolled sheets.
Punnet: small basket usually holding 250g fruit.

Rice Bubbles: rice crispies.
Rice Cakes: light and crunchy cakes made from puffed rice, 10cm in diameter.
Rockmelon: cantaloupe.

ROYAL ICING
1 egg white
1¾ cup icing sugar
1 teaspoon lemon juice

Place egg white in a small bowl, lightly beat with a fork. Add sifted icing sugar a tablespoon at a time and beat well between each addition, until icing holds stiff peaks. Add lemon juice and colouring.

SAUCES:

Soy: made from fermented soy beans; we used light and and dark varieties. The light is generally used with white meat dishes, and the darker variety with red meat dishes. The dark is normally used for colour and the light for flavour.
Tomato: tomato ketchup.
Sesame Seeds: we used the white variety. To toast: spread seeds evenly onto oven tray, toast in moderate oven for about 5 minutes.
Shallots, Green: also known as scallions or spring onions; do not confuse with the small golden shallots.
Shortcrust Pastry: basic pastry using half the amount of shortening (butter or margarine) to flour. Frozen shortcrust pastry is available in sheets from supermarkets.
Shortcrust Pastry Cases: we used Pampas frozen Sweet Shortcrust Tart Cases (12 in 275g packet).
Smarties: multi-coloured sweets with milk chocolate centres.
Soft Icing: ready-to-use cake fondant available in 500g packets and 375g tubs; the tubs are labelled "prepared icing".
Soup Mix, Dry: sold in sachets, available in a range of flavours.
Sponge Rollettes: we used small sponge rolls about 9cm long filled with jam or jam and cream; these are generally purchased in 250g packets of 6.
Sprinkles: different coloured cake sprinkles (nonpareils).
SUGAR:
Castor: fine granulated table sugar.
Crystal: granulated table sugar.

Icing: confectioners' or powdered sugar. We used icing sugar mixture, not pure.
Sweets: we used a large variety of readily available sweets and other edible goodies. Use photographs as a guide to what to buy. Most commerical sweets and biscuits, etc, recommended in this book are described alphabetically.

Tomato Paste: a concentrated tomato puree used as a flavouring in soups and sauces.

Vanilla Essence: we used imitation extract.

VIENNA CREAM
125g (4oz) butter
1 ½ cups icing sugar

Have butter at room temperature, place butter in small bowl of elecric mixer, beat until butter is as white as possible. Gradually add the sifted icing sugar, beating constantly. Colouring should thin the mixture, if mixture is too thick to spread evenly, add milk.

Wafers: thin crisp biscuits generally served with ice-cream and creamy desserts, can also be layered with sweet cream filling.
White Chocolate Melts: compounded white chocolate discs 2 .5cm in diameter.

Zucchini: courgette.

HOW TO MAKE PATTERNS FROM OUR DIAGRAMS

Take a large sheet of paper and draw in right angles or border lines using a dressmaker's ruler. Measure from angles to points for pattern piece, draw in straight lines. To draw a curve at sleeve, armhole, neckline etc, mark in border lines then hold a tape measure on its side at the correct length for curve, between the border lines. Move the tape measure between border lines to achieve the desired curve, maintaining the correct length. Draw in the curve and check by remeasuring. Slight adjustments may be necessary; scoop out the curve a little more to make it larger, or fill the curve in to make it smaller.

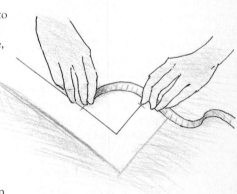

CUTTING OUT
Cutting directions on diagrams (Cut 2 etc) refer to main fabric only; directions for cutting lining, wadding and interfacing are given in the first paragraph of instructions.

SIZES
Patterns are sized to fit the age range of the party. Check pattern pieces against your child and make adjustments, if necessary, before cutting fabric.

VARIATIONS
Use our jumpsuit and hood patterns as basics, and add extras to create the costumes you desire. Our Louie the Lion costume could easily be converted into a Grizzly Bear suit – just change the shape of the ears and tail. The Alien could just as easily be transformed into a slinky Catsuit, just add ears and a tail.

Cup and Spoon Measurements

To ensure accuracy in your recipes use the standard metric measuring equipment approved by Standards Australia:
(a) 250 millilitre cup for measuring liquids. A litre jug *(capacity 4 cups)* is also available.
(b) a graduated set of four cups – measuring 1 cup, half, third and quarter cup – for items such as flour, sugar, etc. When measuring in these fractional cups, level off at the brim.
(c) a graduated set of four spoons: tablespoon *(20 millilitre liquid capacity)*, teaspoon *(5 millilitre)*, half and quarter teaspoons. The Australian, British and American teaspoon each has 5ml capacity.

Approximate cup and spoon conversion chart

Australian	American & British
1 cup	1¼ cups
¾ cup	1 cup
⅔ cup	¾ cup
½ cup	⅔ cup
⅓ cup	½ cup
¼ cup	⅓ cup
2 tablespoons	¼ cup
1 tablespoon	3 teaspoons

All spoon measurements are level.

Note: NZ, USA and UK all use 15ml tablespoons.

We have used large eggs with an average weight of 60g each in all recipes.

OVEN TEMPERATURES

Electric	C°	F°
Very slow	120	**250**
Slow	150	300
Moderately slow	160-180	325-350
Moderate	180-200	375-400
Moderately hot	210-230	425-450
Hot	240-250	475-500
Very hot	260	525-550

Gas	C°	F°
Very slow	120	250
Slow	150	300
Moderately slow	160	325
Moderate	180	350
Moderately hot	190	375
Hot	200	400
Very hot	230	450

INDEX